Art of the South African Townships

206

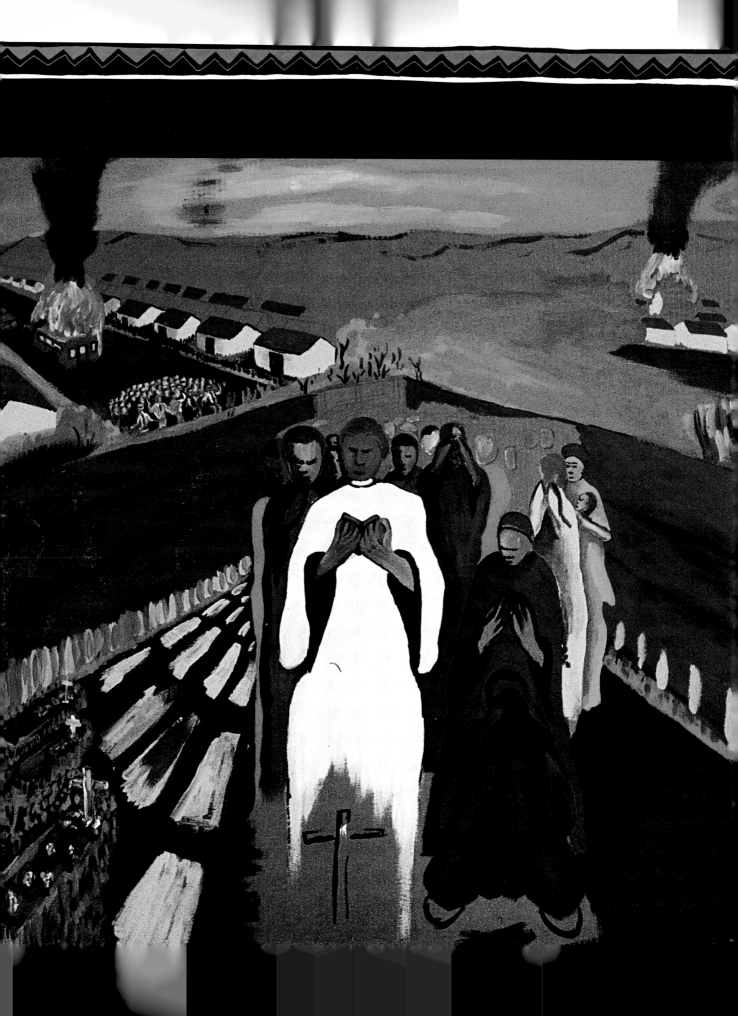

Gavin Younge

Art of the South African Townships

Foreword by Archbishop Desmond M. Tutu

with 134 illustrations, 100 in colour

Thames and Hudson

Frontispiece: *Guguletu,* acrylic on corrugated cardboard, Boyskin Sipoko, 1976.

© 1988 Thames and Hudson Ltd, London
Photographs © 1988 Gavin Younge

Contents

Foreword by the Most Reverend Desmond M. Tutu, D.D., F.K.C.
Anglican Archbishop of Cape Town

We who have been formed by the prevailing consumer society always want to put a price on things. We want to be told whether something has a practical use or not and, depending on the answer, we either value or disdain whatever, or whoever, was in question. Most of us have become victims of utilitarianism and unquestioning adherents of consumerism.

But what commercial value can we attach to a beautiful flower? What about a breathtaking view such as that of Table Mountain with its wisps of mist and cloud forming the proverbial tablecloth – what value can we ever attach to them except that they are beautiful and that we would be impoverished without them. Beauty is self-authenticating and self-justifying.

When the San painted their exquisite rock paintings, they did so because they believed that these gave them power in the hunt. But the power they received from these paintings was the power of the knowledge that to be human is to be creative as well. Art, poetry, music, literature, all testify to the fact that we are more than just creatures of our environment, creatures of flesh and the blood we have inside us.

This can be a subversive claim in the face of injustice and oppression and all that would turn human beings into counters to be manipulated, to be pushed and shoved, here and there, as if they had not been created in the image of God.

Art of the South African Townships contains examples of art which make such a claim and which speak about noble things. Art which shows that we are made for other things than to be denizens of the fetid squalor of the ghetto. Art which shows that, despite everything to the contrary, we do not live by bread alone.

This art is in large measure a protest against race-obsessed bureaucrats who like to classify people into neat little packages, but who are nonetheless smart enough to ban cultural events because they know that culture can undermine racist exploitative ideology. Through art, and through creativity, blacks can transcend the claustrophobia of their physical environment. They could as easily not engage in artistic activity as not breathe. This art, and we are grateful to Gavin Younge for this thoughtful compilation, affirms that blacks are human and that one day they too will be free from all that seeks to make them less than this.

Cape Town, 1988

6

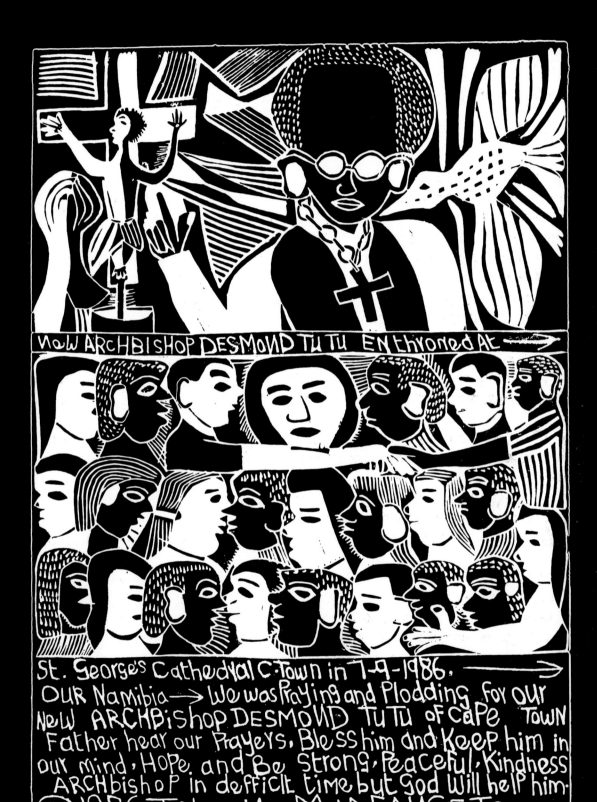

New ARCHBISHOP DESMOND TUTU ENThroned At →

St. George's Cathedral C.Town in 7-9-1986. →
OUR Namibia → We was Praying and Plodding for our
New ARCHBiShoP DESMOND TuTU of caPe TOWN
Father hear our Prayers, Bless him and Keep him in
our mind, Hope. and Be strong, Peaceful, Kindness
ARCHbishoP in deffIcIt time byt God Will helP him.
© 1986 John N. MUAFANGEJO

Author's Preface

This book is concerned with the present state of art in the black townships of South Africa. Though very little has been published about this important body of work, many people, on the evidence of what is illustrated here, will undoubtedly be astonished that this urban black art has not found wider exposure.

This study began as a series of lectures in the course that I teach at the University of Cape Town. Finding very few examples of black art in our photographic library, and none at all in the Union Library, I began to document work whenever the opportunity presented itself. The first fruitful opportunity grew out of a film project in the Ntlaveni area with a social historian, Patrick Harries. We abandoned our project soon after starting it in 1984, but I stayed on and visited two sculptors, Nelson Mukhuba and Jackson Hlungwani. Although the visual authority of their work seemed to demonstrate direct continuity with traditional African carving, I was struck by the fact that they had both spent the larger portion of their lives working in the cities and that their work voiced this experience in a remarkable way.

The following year I undertook an extended field trip with a group of students. Sensing that many artists had not exhibited in galleries, we relied on contacts provided by individuals and organizations. Where possible, appointments were made beforehand to visit particular artists in their homes. At a time when many of the townships were sealed off by the police, 'MK' Malefane arranged for Soweto-based artists to visit us in town. Likewise, Paul Sibisi's generosity in showing us the work of other artists at the Port Natal beer hall was characteristic of the openness and sense of collaboration I have found throughout the period spent working on this project. At the end of 1986, I was fortunate in being able to employ Luthando Lupuwana as a graduate research assistant. Our discussions helped to refine my understanding of the deeply symbolic approach favoured by many artists in a political situation which seemed to demand more direct participation and action.

Although art is often written about in the context of specific geographic 'schools', such as 'Bloomsbury', 'East Village' and so on, the term 'township art' is offensive to some artists and stylistically indefensible. However, segregated residential areas are still a legal requirement in South Africa and it seems therefore appropriate to focus on the townships as a site of mobilization for the development of a 'new' South African culture. These ideas are assessed in a chapter which examines the forms of township development and their part in controlling not only African urbanization, but also African nationalism. It is also hoped that the essays on township development and black art training during the period of 'Bantu Education', the involvement of the churches and the subsequent rise of community-based educational initiatives will help to set the thematic richness and variety of urban black art in its proper context.

The controls imposed by the South African Government failed to curb either black urbanization or nationalism, and much of the art produced in the townships is a unique commentary on this failure. Often, this art is wrought from poor, or discarded materials. In the overcrowded and poverty-stricken townships, this fact is not a matter of choice. Africa's artists have never depended on expensive art materials.

Surprisingly, in the same way that many black writers continue to express themselves in the language of the 'oppressor', English or Afrikaans, so too a number of artists have mastered so-called 'Western' techniques. This work challenges the received notions of what is authentic 'African' art and what is not. The process of transformation, whether it be from the 'traditional' to the 'modern', or from the 'subjugated' to the 'liberated', requires the insights of those capable of matching evolving forms of human association to cultural and social continuities. Some of the work reproduced in these pages does this magnificently.

No particular structure has been intended by the sequence of work in the section on individual artists. The stylistic and situational similarities which seemed to group the work of the muralists, Emily Motsoeneng and Melita Molokwane, seemed justification for keeping the entries on the sculptors, Seoka and Maswanganyi, separate. Urban/rural classifications are rendered false by the migrant labour system which, together with taxation and the further collapse of 'homeland' agriculture, inexorably controls the movement of people in and out of the industrial areas. Even the yardstick of art training is rendered spurious by the fact that, although Motsoeneng and others did not attend art school, they were nonetheless taught how to paint. As a force for communication, the internal consistencies of the work of artists as different as Mnyele and Ngumo transcend any categories that can be established by comparing their work. Rather, we are left with the larger political categories of their dispossession and their martyrdom.

Gavin Younge
Cape Town, 1988

'Culture within our struggle'
Township Art and Politics

It will undoubtedly come as a surprise to many people that any art at all has surfaced through the bleak, dusty streets and urban squalor of the South African townships. The world at large is perhaps aware that the township residents queue for buses long before dawn and return home well after sunset to houses which often do not have the convenience of electric light. There seems little time or space for creative pursuits. It is therefore even more surprising that the work celebrated in this book should prove to be of such sustained quality and complexity.

Yet this art cannot be understood or appreciated without some knowledge of the artist's position within the townships and within the political struggle currently taking place in South Africa. At this point in time, many younger artists no longer have faith in the power of subtle, elusive and surprising art forms and either retire their talents or submerge them in organizational work. The promise of art as a form of human communication which is visually, emotionally and, at the very least, intellectually satisfying, has

been side-lined by the urgency of a social and political situation where children are detained, parents shot and collaborators burned. In fact, the status of the township artists as artists had eventually become so diminished that a number of anti-apartheid organizations and unions decided to reappraise the role of the creative arts within their struggle. The cultural co-ordinator of COSATU (Congress of South African Trade Unions) has remarked that 'the problem in the past has . . . . never been given enough prominence within democratic organizations'. A pamphlet, *To All Organizations and Cultural Workers*, published on the occasion of the 1986 Cape Town Arts Festival, broached the issue directly: 'Organizations have been reawakened to the importance of culture within our struggle and the need to assert people's culture.'

This book concerns itself essentially with the emergence of that culture in the visual art of the townships. These segregated residential areas have been a fundamental feature of apartheid policy since the 1950s and the physical

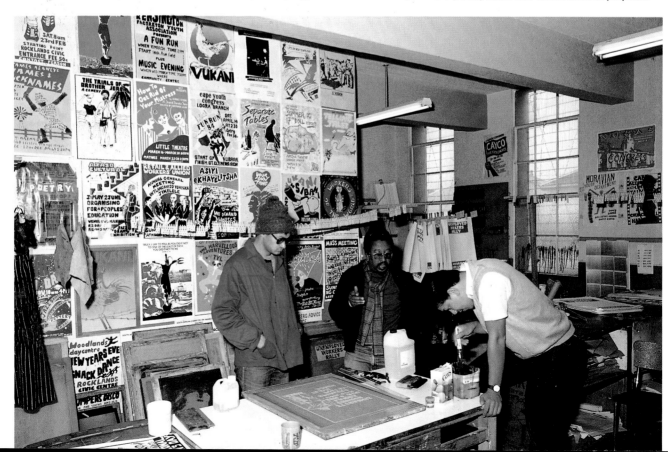

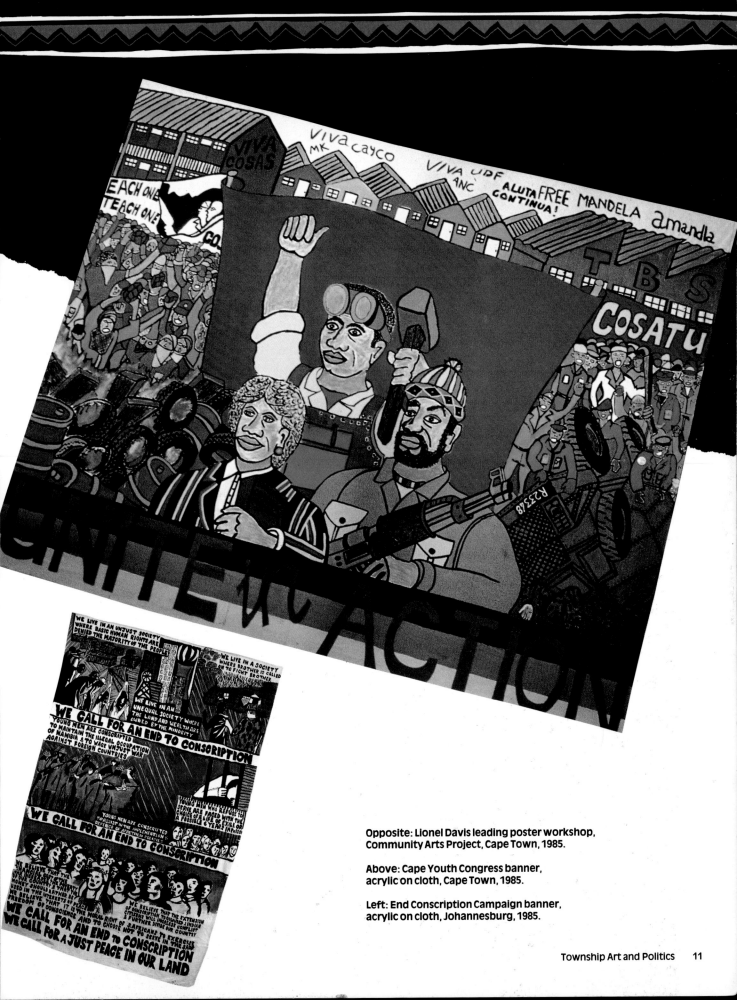

Opposite: Lionel Davis leading poster workshop, Community Arts Project, Cape Town, 1985.

Above: Cape Youth Congress banner, acrylic on cloth, Cape Town, 1985.

Left: End Conscription Campaign banner, acrylic on cloth, Johannesburg, 1985.

layout of all South African towns, without exception, is articulated by the apartheid ideal of separation. Despite decades of resistance, this ideal is still being energetically pursued by government planners. The form of South African towns, with their neatly laid-out white suburbs and sprawling black townships, conditions every aspect of daily life. It would seem that no human interaction can escape the blight of an ideology which is lived out on such civic proportions. However, many artists have tried to do just that; to reach out towards each other across the gulf of entrenched inequality and racist legislation; to transcend apartheid on the only plane which appears possible, that is, on a personal level.

This book includes some of those brave efforts at building bridges through the medium of art. It also includes the work of artists who believe that art has an important role to play in ending apartheid. Not only in pictures of defiance, the clenched fist and mass rally, but in a committed art which affirms human dignity, compassion and intelligence in an overall programme which is aimed at majority rule.

The origins of this study lie in the author's friendship with two sculptors living some distance apart in the northern Transvaal, Nelson Mukhuba and Jackson Hlungwani. Both these artists worked in manufacturing industry as migrant labourers before becoming artists. It took them both more than twenty years to reject the pitiless system of contract

labour and to restart their careers as artists. They had no savings, no contacts, not even a refuge in bitterness. All they had was a deeply felt sense of human dignity and that strangely egotistical determination common to all artists.

The world may have heard of Soweto and Sebokeng, but in hundreds of smaller townships with names like Ezakheni and Elukhanyisweni, Mbekweni and Zwelithemba, street committees have built up powerful organizational networks around the day-to-day issues of township life. These organizations, known by a bewildering array of acronyms (CAP, CAHAC, CAYCO, WECTU, NECC), have taken the 'struggle' into every school and most households. In an attempt to counter the increasingly organized character of black resistance, the South African Government acted against seventeen of these organizations in February 1988. The National Education Crisis Committee (NECC) and the United Democratic Front (UDF) were, to all intents and purposes, banned from further operations.

This crackdown follows the imposition of the second State of Emergency in June 1986 and highlights the new-found strength of community organizations. In recent years, many artists have allied themselves to these organizations and have tried not only to reflect political issues in their work, but to build effective structures through which a non-racial South African culture can be developed. Although the townships were originally part of the state's strategy to

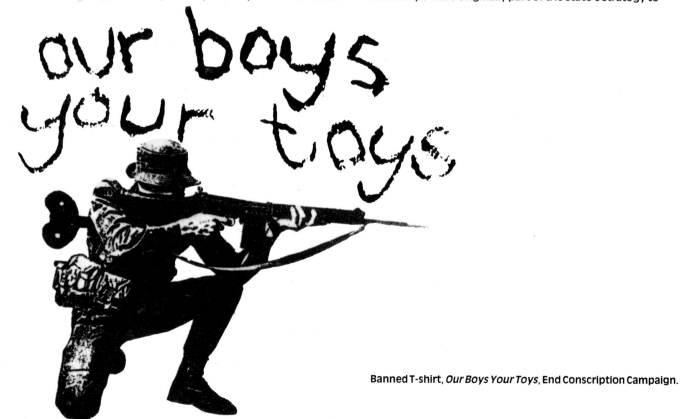

Banned T-shirt, *Our Boys Your Toys*, End Conscription Campaign.

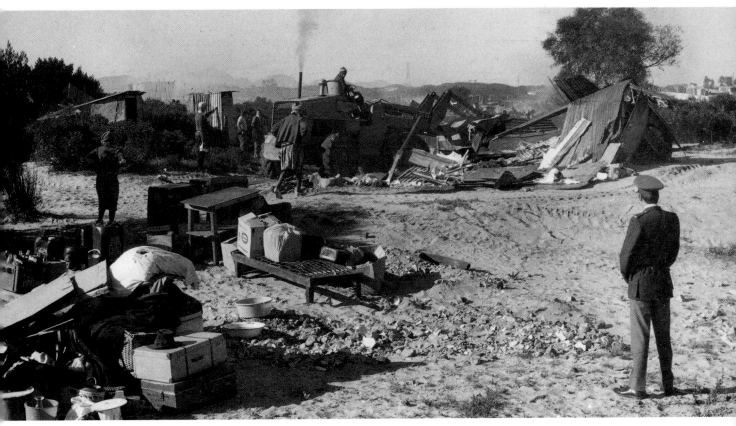

Forced removals from vacant land in Belville South, Cape Town, August 1977.

create an exclusively black working class, they have now become important arenas in the struggle against apartheid structures. It is therefore appropriate that a study of contemporary black art should examine, at least in outline, the history of the state's housing and educational strategies as applied to the black community.

The interpretation of any art involves questions of cultural signification and social legitimation; in other words, questions of ideology. While it may be readily admitted that colonial powers in the past tended to undervalue grossly the cultural achievements of indigenous peoples, the legacy of that phenomenon is now less readily admitted. Doors which have been closed for decades have now been thrown open. Exhibition curators and museum administrators make every effort to include work by black artists, but mistrust and the fear that their participation will confer an appearance of legitimacy on existing establishment structures keep most black artists away.

However, terms such as 'black art' themselves present problems. South Africa is locked in a broad-based struggle to free itself of a particularly vicious form of institutionalized racism and any mention of racial categories is immediately suspect: the word 'black' is no longer simply an adjective – it has become a political term. As desirable as it may be, the ideal of a 'South African art', one which is unmarked by racial categorization, cannot be achieved by simply ignoring the imprint of racist legislation which is still very much in force. In *I Write What I Like*, the late Steve Biko wrote that 'modern African culture emanates from a situation of common experience of oppression.' It would be premature to write about the character of South African art as a whole before these structures of oppression have been removed.

The art of Africa has changed. The tribal past, glorified in the glossy pages of African art magazines, presents a view of African art as European collectors would like to see it. Unchanging and uncontaminated by Western influence, this art attests to its irreplaceable value by the irrevocable passing of its vanquished cultures. In South Africa, as in the rest of Africa, this art has been borne away by missionaries, tourists and returning functionaries. Sometimes sold and sometimes bartered, it is difficult not to feel that the social and religious impetus for this art has been buried in the museum cases along with the works themselves and that the artistic impulse of South Africa is dead.

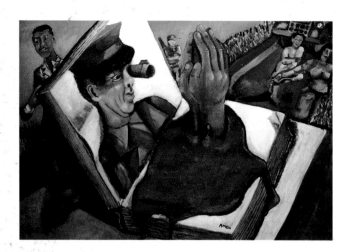

Above: untitled, oil on canvas, Eunice Sefaka, 1986.

Opposite: *Nelson Mandela*, oil on canvas, 'M K' Malefane, *c*.1983. This portrait of her husband hung in the house in Brandfort to which Winnie Mandela had been banished. The painting was destroyed in a fire-bomb attack on her home in 1985.

Below: *Slugabed*, oil paint on fibreglass resin laminate, Michele Raubenheimer, 1985. This work was accepted with misgivings by the curator of the Shell Gallery in Johannesburg for exhibition as part of the University of the Witwatersrand's post-graduate show. Acting on public complaints, the Publications Control Board declared the sculpture 'undesirable' and told the gallery to remove it from public view. Rather than censor part of the exhibition, the organizers decided to close the whole exhibition.

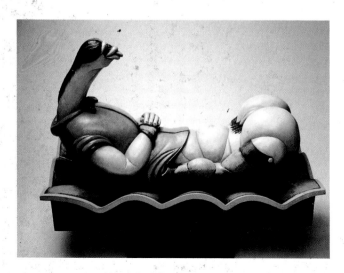

This book is a testimony to the unfounded character of that supposition. The works of art reproduced in these pages are more than the reflections of socio-cultural structures; they embody and actively participate in those structures. They also represent the artists' views of themselves in a shifting urban environment which embraces evolving forms of human association. The 'men only' beer halls, the shebeens, stokvel parties, labour offices and church halls all impose conflicting expectations on those who, as artists, must also contend with galleries and selection committees. As a force for communication these works of art hold their own against examples from anywhere in the world.

To many Africans, the process of modernization appears to hold out the promise of emancipation from white domination. Current art reveals that traditional patterns of thought have given way to uniquely reflexive perspectives on the process of African urbanization. The Congress of South African Trade Unions has formed a Cultural Unit and has set about providing workers with video programmes on workers' struggles. Other unions maintain links with community-based arts organizations and produce their own plays and posters. This movement away from ethnically defined culture and the building up of progressive and democratic structures is deeply menacing to the state. Ironically, the tribalism which had posed such a threat to previous colonial and imperial powers is now being fostered by the South African Government through the homeland structures. The sequel to this concern for ethnicity is now being played out, with tragic results, in the struggles between the Zulu cultural organization, Inkatha, and the United Democratic Front.

It is clear that the South African Government is threatened by what it likes to call the 'revolutionary climate' within South Africa and the regulations promulgated by the second State of Emergency enforce new definitions of what comprises a 'subversive statement'. Section One of the act (the Public Safety Act of 1953) makes provision for any picture, photograph, print, engraving, lithograph, painting or drawing, and subsequent sub-sections spell out what is meant by subversion. The provisions of the act are so wide that even the publication of blank spaces where material has been edited out can be considered subversive. Protests as ephemeral as those emblazoned on T-shirts have been considered subversive and have been banned. In 1987 a farm labourer, Benjamin de Bruyn, appeared in court on charges under the Internal Security Act. The charges related to a number of tattoos on his body, one of which read 'God give me freedom but the whites take it away that's why I an [sic] ANC'. He was ordered to have the tattoos removed and was sentenced to an effective three years imprisonment. Work by

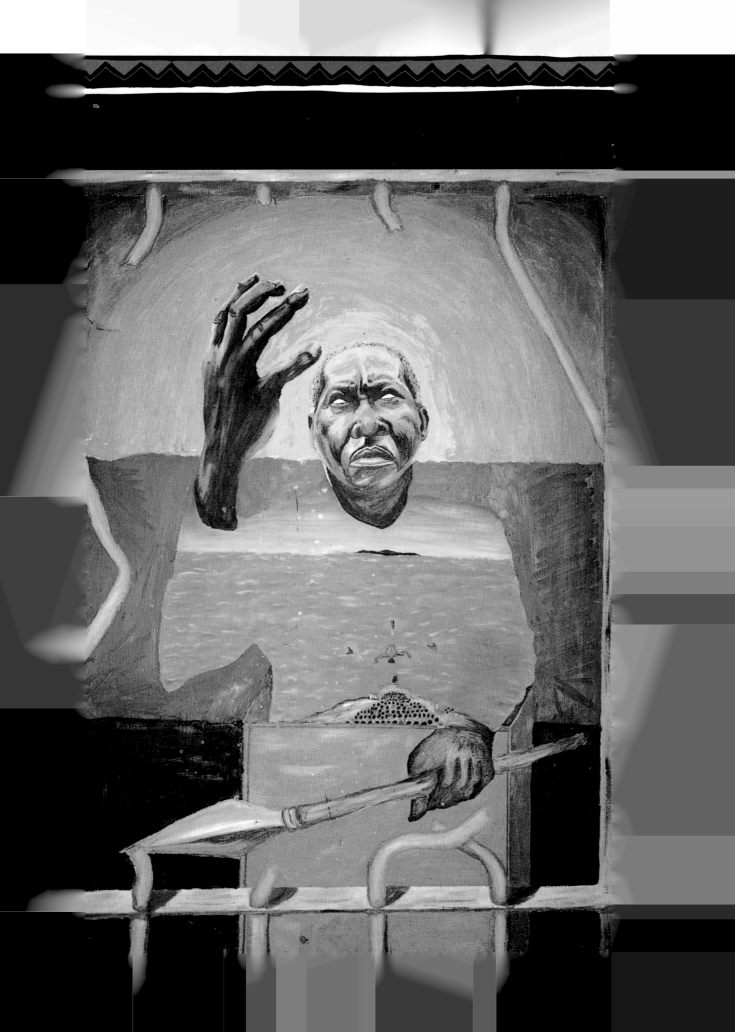

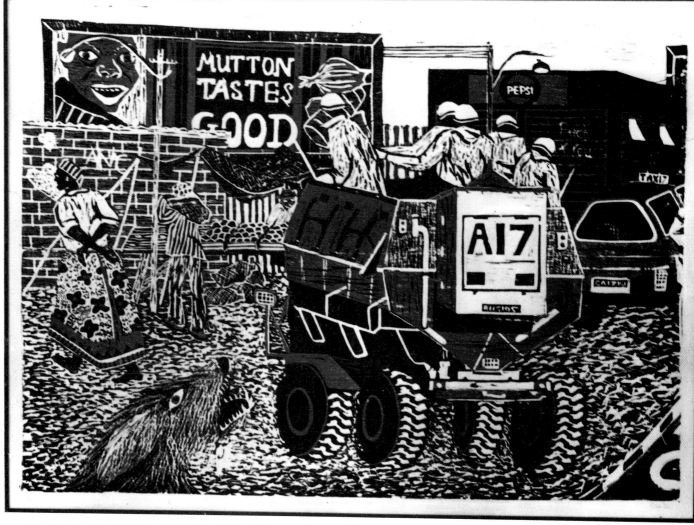

Washington Street, Langa, woodblock relief print, Suzanne Louw, 1986.

artists such as Manfred Zilla, Paul Stopforth, Jonathan Berndt and Michele Raubenheimer have all, in different ways, fallen foul of the intricacies of a system which is as unreliable as it is harsh.

As we have seen earlier in this chapter, the submersion of the township artists in the political struggle did eventually lead to calls for a revaluation of the role of art within that struggle. These calls follow on from the resolutions of the historic Culture and Resistance Symposium which was held in Gaborone in July 1982. More recently, in December 1987, these calls have been given active implementation in the Culture in Another South Africa (CASA) conference which was held in Amsterdam. The success or failure of these strategies does not depend solely on artists. The South African Government banned the Cape Town Arts Festival in its

entirety and is likely to act against any further attempts to democratize culture.

Many pieces in the 1986 Cape Town Arts Festival exhibition offered trenchant satire and protest. However, the exhibition was banned before it opened and it is likely that the authorities were more concerned with the overarching aim of the festival, that is, the building up of people's culture, than with the individual works on exhibition.

Many individual artists directly document the contemporary state of siege in the townships. Billy Mandindi's raw and emblematic image of a 'necklace' victim inside a camouflaged tower engages uneasily with an exhibition audience. Made out of scrap wooden and metal materials, the construction belies its macabre message. The grill covering the aperture of the tower is a clear reference to the wire-meshed windows of police vehicles and identifies the occupant as a collaborator. Despite this polemical attitude, the piece offers a cautionary warning about the finality of 'people's justice'.

Suzanne Louw's series of woodcuts entitled *Washington Street, Langa* display a familiarity with township life which suggests that the artist has either worked from photographs or that she has been a frequent and accepted visitor to the townships. Louw does not work from photographs. The 'documentary' quality of the prints conveys the implication that they are concerned with arousing an active response to the conditions they describe. Their exhibition in Cape Town, both in the Towards a People's Culture exhibition and the University of Cape Town's year-end student exhibition (where they won an award) contravened emergency regulations which specifically outlaw the publicization of police and defence force action without prior approval.

The strident 'Africanist' imagery of much black art has been identified as a feature of political oratory since the 1950s. Tom Lodge, an authority on the history of the African National Congress (ANC), writes (in *Working Papers in South African Studies*, vol. 3, ed. Hindson, Ravan, Johannesburg, 1983) that this imagery, with its frequent themes of martyrdom and sacrifice, came to the fore through ANC Youth League leaders. These themes are evident in 'MK' Malefane's portrait of Nelson Mandela. In this painting, which was destroyed after Winnie Mandela's house at Brandfort was fire-bombed in 1985, the artist has tried to represent the two-fold nature of the struggle by the use of explicit symbolism. One hand is raised in an oratorical gesture while the other is shown holding a spear, symbol of the armed struggle. Despite its melodrama and technical weaknesses, this painting succeeded in reaching black viewers because of its uncompromising acceptance of the necessity of the armed struggle. Mandela's shirt has become a seascape in which the image of a swimmer (Mandela was imprisoned on Robben Island) is menaced by sharks which approach from the four cardinal points of the compass. In this way the artist hopes to draw attention to the South African Government's international allies.

Another aspect of 'Africanist' imagery is evident in the work of Eunice Sefaka. Measured against the outlook of the artist and that of her peers, this melodramatic imagery takes its place in a narrative structure which depends on overstatement. In Sefaka's painting this declamatory tone is evident in the unambiguous use of key symbols. The idea of reconciliation, symbolized here by the Bible and by hands held up in a gesture of prayer, is violently contradicted by the

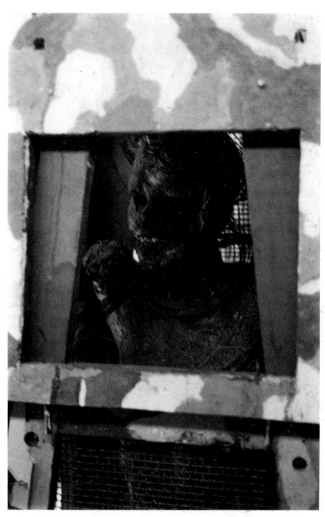

Necklace of Death, mixed media, Billy Mandindi, 1986.

image of a police sharp-shooter. Her overt imagery contrasts strongly with work by Peter Clarke, whose well-crafted images of urban poverty have earned him an international reputation. Similarly, Sam Nhlengethwa's collages convey the dense congestion and vitality of street life, but do not detect the shadow cast by the armed security patrols. For younger artists such as Sefaka, the sheer numbers of people killed in the townships have meant literally that death has become an image of life in the townships.

The closed book of township life is seldom penetrated by the casual visitor. Terms such as 'squalor', 'hardship', or even 'housing', 'recreation' and 'schooling', tend to fragment our understanding of one of the modern world's most calculated attempts at social engineering. These terms may be able to give us endless statistics but they cannot measure subjective experience and a people's resolve to change.

'The doors of learning'
Art Training and 'Bantu Education'

Attempts to use culture in defining 'ethnic identity' have been deeply divisive in the South African educational system; we should now look at the role of art training within the overall structure of what was officially known until 1979 as 'Bantu Education'. Almost inevitably, though, the question of education and the place of art within it leads us back to the social and political context. The schools of the townships offer blacks an arena in which to organize. In the politicized and volatile atmosphere of the school yards students have planned consumer boycotts and other community action

Umzavela Unrest, pen and ink wash on paper, Paul Sibisi, 1981.

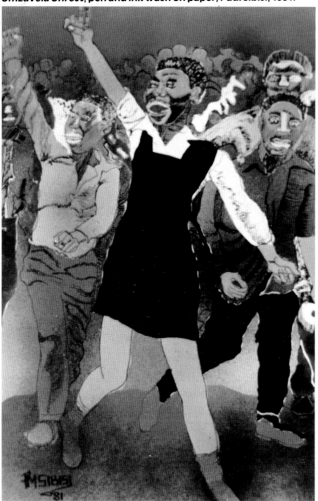

against companies with poor labour records; they have also set about replacing the hated system of Bantu Education with 'People's Education', the seeds of which are contained in a central tenet of the Freedom Charter adopted in 1955: 'The doors of learning and culture shall be opened to all.'

In the present circumstances, however, it is certain that black artists have little or no access to formalized art teaching in the townships. But this may not necessarily be seen as the most pressing deficiency in the circumstances: the artists of Africa have never had much use for formal art schools, nor specialist art shops selling expensive materials. This is not to say, though, that the present predicament of the artist in the townships is not worth further study; such evaluation requires some knowledge of the historical context of black education in South Africa.

The practice of segregated schooling in South Africa can be traced back to the seventeenth century when separate schools were first established for slave children. It is hardly surprising therefore that when specialized art schools first made their appearance in 1897, these schools only admitted white students. The first 'art' oriented school subject available to blacks made its appearance in 1916 when new regulations introduced 'drawing' into the primary school syllabus in Natal, the Transvaal and the Cape Province. Only twenty-five minutes per week were allocated to this subject and the Orange Free State school syllabus did not offer this subject at all. Industrial work included modelling in clay, sewing and basketwork up to the fourth year of school. Thereafter the subject was differentiated according to gender. Boys were instructed in the 'manipulation of simple tools', and girls were taught 'cooking and simple domestic work'. At the time, and the mission schools were party to this emphasis, the African school curriculum emphasized moral training, punctuality and honesty, manual skills such as woodwork and gardening and, most importantly, a working knowledge of either English or Afrikaans. Basic reading, writing and arithmetic were also taught.

It was against this background that the Nationalist Party formulated an overall educational strategy soon after they were swept into power by white voters in 1948. Following on from the recommendations of the 1951 Eiselin Commission report, the control of African schools was gradually removed from the jurisdiction of the churches and other non-state

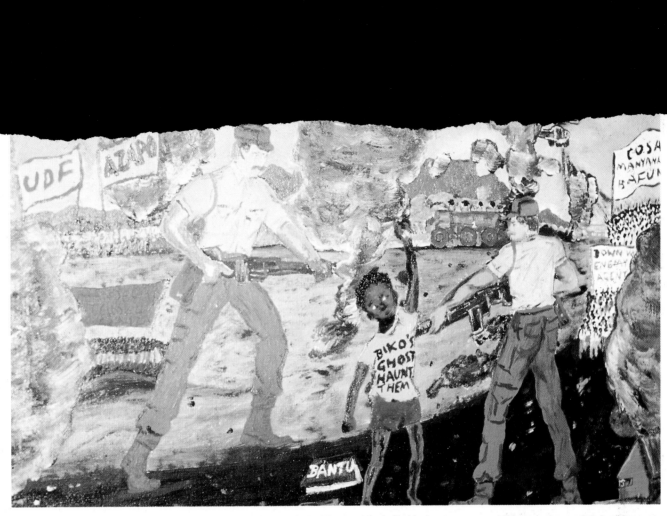

Biko's Ghost Haunt Them . . . , poster paint on paper, Sipho Hlati, 1985. Confrontation between young children and armed riot policemen are common occurrences and Sipho Hlati, who is a student at the Community Arts Project, identifies personally with the arrest of the youth. This arrest, and the child's unrepentant salute, is clearly the dramatic focus of the painting. Painted after the declaration of the first State of Emergency on 21 July 1985, the documentary style of the painting was an attempt to bring 'news' out of the townships at a time when they had been sealed off to newspeople. Despite the painting's strong narrative structure, the 'battle' scene has been mythologized. This is evident in the signposting of different elements of the popular struggle: the struggle against 'Bantu Education', 'enemy agents' and sectarianism. The latter element is evident in the flying of the UDF and AZAPO banners at the same rally. This painting disappeared from the End Conscription Campaign's Art for Peace exhibition at the University of Cape Town in 1985.

bodies. In 1953 there were over 5,000 state-aided mission schools; by 1965 this number had been reduced to 509 out of a total of 7,222 black schools. Teacher training and certification were centralized and placed under party command and all syllabuses were redrawn to conform to standards laid down in Pretoria. Education was removed from the jurisdiction of the four provinces and three separate education departments were created. The Bantu Education Act was passed in 1953 and the Coloured and Indian Education Acts, passed ten years later, sealed off any remaining chinks in the armour of segregated education.

These acts of parliament represent a great deal of strategizing on the part of government planners in order to achieve what was already a firmly established practice, namely, separate schools for white and black. Why then the need for new legislation? Bantu Education was necessary because it completed the pattern of control aimed at the retribalization of black South Africans, while assuring an adequate supply of non-competitive, cheap labour for South African mines and industry. The provisions of Bantu Education, together with other legislation, aimed at stripping, in perpetuity, the majority of Africans of their South African nationality. Realizing that increased repression alone could not halt growing demands for full political rights, Nationalist Party leaders came up with the novel concept of granting independence to pockets of black-owned land in which Africans were henceforward expected to exercise their democratic rights.

Bantu Education, as befitting its central role in this arsenal of new legislation, acted to turn Africans' attention from the urban areas by emphasis on the exclusive, tribal compositions of the schools. Thus, the old-style African schools were replaced by government schools and by so-called 'community schools'. By appointing selected leaders to sit on 'community councils' it was hoped that their power and conservative influence would be strengthened and that tribal antagonisms would be resurrected. This attempt to retribalize the African people, once their military powers had been broken, was a conscious attempt to defuse the growing tide of black nationalism by fostering sectarianism.

Whereas the 'pass laws', labour bureaux, and group areas legislation sought to regulate the movement of Africans, Bantu Education was aimed at dwarfing the minds of black children and so preparing them for a life of servitude. Fears had long been expressed that trouble would result if education gave Africans false expectations; this attitude was now enshrined in official educational policy.

Resistance to Bantu Education, which was formally introduced on April 1955, took the same form as it had previously. Pupils simply stayed away from school. Teachers mounted the first concerted action through the Cape and Transvaal African Teachers' Associations and through the Teachers' League of South Africa. Schools were burnt down at Aliwal North in the Cape and at Bethal in the Transvaal. In Natal, the Ndaleni Industrial School, which had been in existence since the 1850s, was also burnt to the ground. The Government's response also set the pattern for years to come. All 1,054 pupils who boycotted classes at a Zeerust lower-primary school were banned from school for life.

Black art education at the primary school level never received any serious attention until the appointment of J. W. Grossert as Organizer of Arts and Crafts in Natal on 1 August 1948. Under his direction, Arts and Crafts was established as a formalized subject. The declared aim was to revive craft traditions which had been threatened by the availability of Western goods. Classes became more pupil-oriented and schoolchildren regained the self-confidence to represent themselves in their drawings and painting. Teachers who had complained that they could not teach art because they themselves could not 'draw' came to realize that the old method of teaching art, that is, the copying of teacher's drawings off the blackboard, was inappropriate.

The new primary school syllabus, drawn up in 1949, required a degree of proficiency in three languages and emphasized arithmetical skills over handwork and scientific knowledge. The 'handwork' section broke with the carpentry

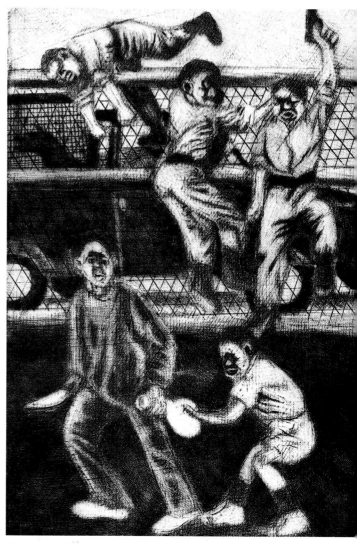

Take Care of the Young, mezzotint, Smart Gumede, 1987.

bias of the previous syllabus. Instead, the pupils' wide knowledge of plants and plant dyes was drawn on and various articles were made in the 'traditional' manner. Realizing that grasses, fibres and sedges were plentiful, the 1949 syllabus (which until 1954 applied only to Natal) included the making of baskets, bowls, bags and mats, woven from the several hundred grass types known to schoolchildren. The Arts and Crafts syllabus was revised in 1956 and again in 1963. The emphasis on so-called traditional crafts was retained and teachers were encouraged to elicit the co-operation of the pupils in the drawing up of the scheme of work.

The lack of distinction between art and craft inherent in this approach is commendable. It is also significant that in a world awash with mass-produced injection-moulded plastic buckets, the 1984 Festival of African Art at the University of Zululand could still exhibit finely stitched *isichumo* beer baskets produced by artists such as Norah Mangela. This is perhaps not solely attributable to the school syllabus, but there appears to be nothing intrinsically wrong about its emphasis on traditional skills and processes.

However, when this emphasis is seen in its overall context of Bantu Education, it is clear that the government schools taught art and craft in isolation from the forces which had jeopardized those craft skills in the first instance. The syllabus is magnificently silent on the history and cultural achievements of the African peoples, let alone the history of resistance to colonial occupation.

Under Verwoerd's administration of Bantu Education there was an increase in the number of schools, particularly of the lower-primary schools. However, this extension of basic education did not result in an improvement of opportunity for Africans, primarily because teacher training standards were dropped dramatically. The school system was broken up into three basic categories and pupils were allowed to leave after the lower-primary stage which was the equivalent of six years of schooling. These children were taught by teachers who themselves had not finished their schooling. Secondly, a system of automatic promotion was introduced. These factors, together with the increase in the pupil-to-teacher ratio, meant that the standard of education actually dropped. In Natal the ratio increased from 40 pupils per teacher to 51 pupils per teacher in the decade 1952-62. Exposure to such rudimentary education could hardly result in mastery of any area and the school-leaver was left with a feeling of inferiority in the company of white school-leavers who had received a free and compulsory school education. Taking expenditure levels in 1960, twenty-five times more money was spent annually on each white school pupil than that spent on each black pupil.

The teaching of art and craft suffered from untrained teachers, poor facilities and, most importantly, the centralization of control in Pretoria. With the passing of the Bantu Education Act in 1953, *all* black schools had to be registered with the Department of Bantu Education and this department had the power to refuse registration or to deregister schools at will. However, the most lasting restraint on the development of creative and expressive skills was the fact that art was never emphasized at secondary school level.

Within the overall mediocrity of educational opportunities available to Africans, the lack of art training facilities is hardly significant. Those initiatives which were mounted all foundered on the scarcity of funds and the first

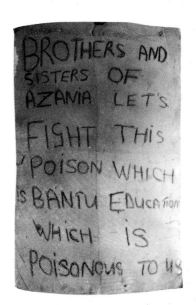

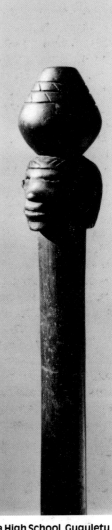

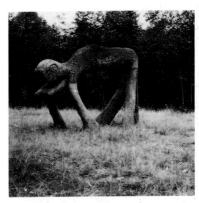

Top: *Brothers and Sisters*, placard, Fezeka High School, Guguletu, Cape Town, 1984.

Above: *Beast*, cement on wire, Ndaleni Teachers' Training College, *c.*1959.

Right above: Shinqhonqani medicine stick. This nineteenth-century example of wood carving was still in use by a traditional healer in the Malamulela area in 1987. Remedies are stored in a hole cut into the vessel on the woman's head.

project to make any impact had its origin in the vicissitudes of the Johannesburg Local Committee for Non-European Adult Education. This committee, through the efforts of people such as Gideon Uys, Reg Rawlings and Father Trevor Huddleston, secured funds from the Union Education Department for the literacy and handicraft classes which were being run at a disused hostel in Polly Street.

Art classes began in 1950 under the guidance of E. K. Lorrimer. Cecil Skotnes, who was already working for the

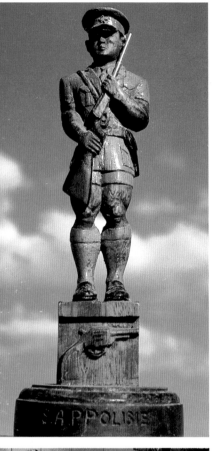

Carving of a South African policeman, enamel paint on wood, artist unknown, photographed in 1985. Commemorative public sculpture can be seen in the streets and parks of most towns. In trying to make articles which will appeal to tourists and passing motorists, woodcarvers have copied stylistic elements from the most readily available examples of 'white' art. In this carving of a burly South African policeman, the heroic stance and plinth are borrowed from the vocabulary of civic statuary.

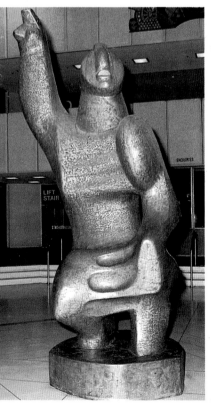

The Blessing, cast bronze, Sydney Kumalo, 1981. This was one of four sculptures commissioned by the City Council for the Cape Town Civic Centre after a nationwide competition. The image of a man crouching, short legs bent at the knee and the right arm raised in a gesture of emphasis, owes much to Kumalo's Polly Street contemporaries. There are genuflections to 'traditional' African art; the mask-like face and the convention of animation conveyed through the legs being bent. Symmetry, with its correlation of elemental opposites, has been dispensed with in favour of dynamism and movement. Although the somewhat spurious embellishment of the 'skirt' and the absorption of the left hand in the main form, recalls the ellipsis of Julian Motau's charcoal drawings, Kumalo is on his own in the treatment of the back. Here his metaphorical associations of man and beast gain primacy over the approbation of the title.

Non-European Affairs Department (NEAD) in Jabavu No. 2 Township, was promoted to the post of Cultural Officer in 1952 and took over responsibility for the Polly Street Art Centre. With the phasing in of Bantu Education in 1953, the Union Education funds and the literacy classes came to an end. The Centre was then run on money raised by renting out the hall to musicians competing in the annual Johannesburg Bantu Music Festival (JBMF). At its inception in the late 1940s, this festival proved extremely popular among urban black South Africans and good relations prevailed between the white civic officials and the performers. As petty apartheid bureaucracy made itself felt this co-operative atmosphere perished and Wilson 'King Force' Silgee remembers that working-class blacks began to see the festival as a place for the 'whites' good boys'.

Skotnes emphasized the notion of professionalism and encouraged students to exhibit, both in the centre's annual exhibition and, if possible, in the galleries. While still a student, Sydney Kumalo worked on sculptural commissions and in 1958 he was appointed Skotnes's assistant and official Art Organizer in the NEAD. Out-reach classes were started in Moroka Township and in 1960 the centre moved to the Jubilee Centre at the Jan Hofmeyr School of Social Work. This centre was adjacent to the Bantu Men's Social Centre (BMSC) and the healthy relationship between urban black performance and visual culture was continued. Artists reasoned that if black playwrights such as James Jolobe could dramatize African working-class life in his production of *Amathunzi Obomi*, then they could achieve the same success and peer group recognition with their paintings of township life. The difference is that, unlike music and theatre, art never achieved the same working-class following. The price of a theatre ticket is in no way commensurate with the price of even the cheapest charcoal drawing and black artists had to seek white buyers for their work. This led to allegations of commercialism and of pandering to what Matsemela Manaka in his book on African art calls, 'self-pity art' (*Echoes of African Art*, Skotaville, 1987).

Another important art centre was established in Natal in the early 1960s. A radio talk, given by the Swedish missionary Helge Fosseus, resulted in the formation of a committee which raised sufficient funds to enable Ulla and Peder Gowenius to come out to South Africa in 1961 and to start a weavery and art school at Umpumulo. Two years later this was moved to the Oskarsberg Mission at Rorke's Drift. The weaving workshop was organized co-operatively and gave employment to local women and helped subsidize the school which was known as the Evangelical Lutheran Church (ELC) Art and Craft Centre. A ceramic workshop, under Kirsten Ollson, was added in 1968.

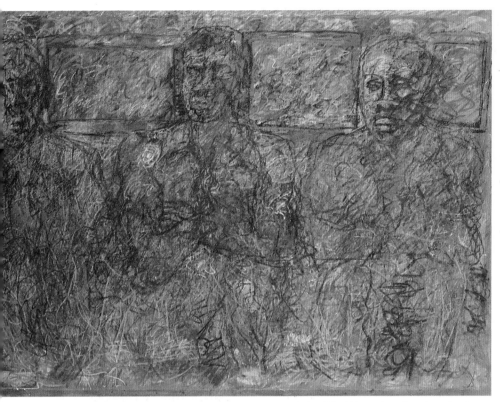

Workers, oil on canvas, David Koloane, 1987. The trace of David Koloane's extensive training, not only at the Bill Ainslie Studios in the mid 1970s, but more recently at the Triangle Workshop in America, is evident in this highly literate painting. He has re-introduced the figure into his scumbled and layered surfaces in deference to the current debate among black artists as to whether abstraction is relevant to black experience or not. He has also completed a Diploma in Museum Studies at the University of London and is presently curator of the Federated Union of Black Arts (FUBA) Gallery in Johannesburg.

An ex-principal of the school, Jay Johnson, has stated that the school and centre were established 'to explore the possibilities of the arts and crafts as a means of livelihood'. With this aim in mind the organizers have, perhaps not surprisingly, identified west Europeans as their potential market. This has led the weavery to concentrate on luxury wall and floor coverings using the finest wools and mohair. The weavers are responsible for the design and choice of colour and over the years a tradition of figurative tapestries with a strong autobiographical and narrative structure has evolved.

The largely foreign market and the fact that the weavery has not oriented itself towards a 'village industry' producing blankets and other locally useful goods has prompted allegations that the centre is organized along neo-colonial lines. The school has

Far left: Tshogholo ceremonial apron. Glass beads, brass chainmail, linen thread and sinew on goat skin, name of artist not known, 1950s. Glass beads were introduced into the area now known as the Transvaal in the sixteenth century. Trade routes traversed the continent, but the AmaNdebele probably obtained beads from the Portuguese on the Catembé River.

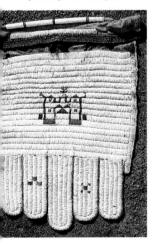

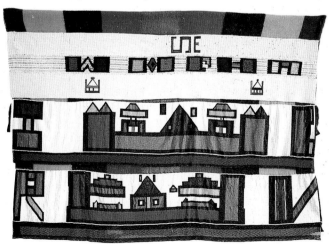

Left: Ngurara ceremonial beaded blanket, glass beads on cotton thread and blanket, name of artist not known, *c.*1960. Dating beadwork presents problems because women sometimes remove panels from older garments and attach them to a new backing or restring them entirely. In this example, the upper strip is made of smaller beads and is probably older than the rest of the beadwork. Attempts by some researchers to construct a colour symbolism have been repudiated. White beads are more expensive than some other colours and recently the representational elements, evident here in the depictions of houses, have become larger in relationship to the white 'ground'. Architectural and other motifs are seldom representations of particular homesteads but are amalgamations of imagined and observed reality.

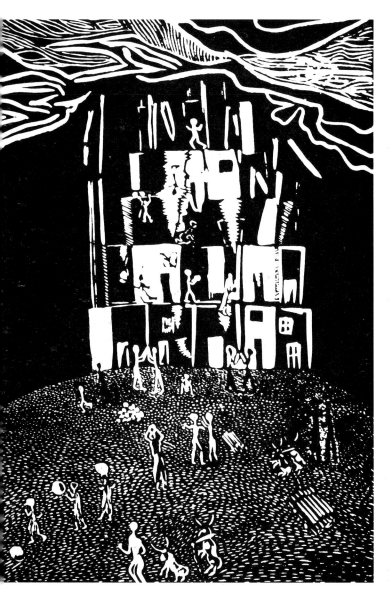

Rise and Destruction of Power, linoleum relief print, Bongiwe Dhlomo, 1981. After working at the Durban African Arts Centre and FUBA, Bongiwe (Bongi) Dhlomo took up the position of co-ordinator at the Alexandra Art Centre in 1986. In this print, a man falls through floorboards which 'cannot hold', while antlike figures play with a beach ball, plough and converse on a vast, geoid-shaped lawn.

faced financial difficulties and the principal, Goran Skogland, was forced to close it temporarily at the end of 1982. However, in its twenty years of operation a number of young artists have successfully completed the two- and three-year Fine Art Certificate.

Together with Azaria Mbatha, John Muafangejo is probably the best-known of these students and both have enjoyed international exposure and acclaim. Other students have become teachers. Anthony Nkotsi now teaches printmaking at the Johannesburg Art Foundation; Lionel Davis teaches at the Community Arts Project in Cape Town, and Velile Soha teaches at the Nyanga Arts Centre. Paul Sibisi, who studied at Rorke's Drift in 1973 and 1974, won a British Council bursary in 1987 and is now a language teacher at the Umzuvela High School in Umlazi, Durban.

Despite the achievements of these and other artists, the visual arts are not seen as an important sector of the economy and government initiatives in the field of tertiary education have been placed elsewhere. It has been said that the emphasis on schools in the lower-primary level provided industry with an oversupply of numerate and literate workers who could understand instructions in the employer's language. This carried obvious benefits to employers in industry and the mines. However, South Africa also suffered from a shortage of skilled technicians in all sectors. This shortage has not been adequately met by the various African-language universities and colleges which were hastily set up after the established universities were closed to blacks in 1959.

The University of Fort Hare at Alice in Ciskei is the oldest tertiary institute for blacks and in 1964 the Department of African Studies established a permanent gallery for the display of the university's extensive collection of contemporary African art. This led to the formation of a Fine Arts department in 1971.

Since the uprising of 1976, organized capital has campaigned loudly and publicly for educational reform. Although Bantu Education did make provision for the training of an élite, this was always conceived in terms of professionals who would cater to the black community 'in their own areas'. In the 1980s big business has needed more than skilled workers on its payroll. Public relations efforts and the divestment lobby have created an urgent need for black managers as well. The reform initiative was officially begun in 1979, three years after Hector Pietersen was shot dead in Soweto. Pietersen was the first of several hundred school-children killed during 1976 as townships across the country erupted in outraged anger at the way in which the authorities had dealt with peaceful protests against the compulsory use of Afrikaans as a medium of instruction in state schools. The vehemence of the resistance led to the banning of eighteen organizations in 1979 and the hated Bantu Education Act was replaced by the Education and Training Bill.

In 1986, school boycotts and the state's reaction in sending army patrols into the schools so disrupted schooling that final school examinations in South Africa's largest black city, Soweto, had to be called off. The only Sowetan

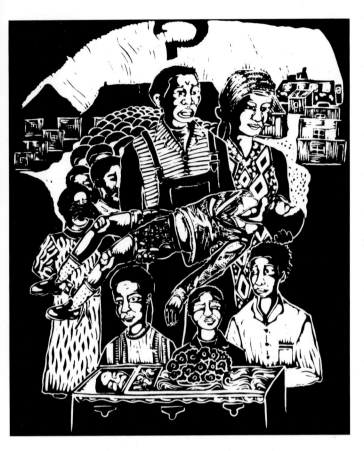

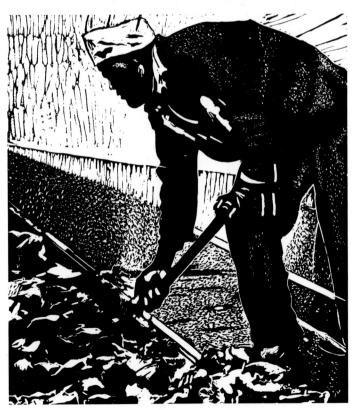

Left: *Hector Pietersen*, linoleum relief print, Sydney Holo, 1982.

Left below: *Railway Worker*, linoleum relief print, Velile Soha, 1986. Asked which artists he admires, Soha singles out Michelangelo and local artists, Esrom Legae and Mpathi Gocini. Soha studied art part-time at the Community Arts Project in 1979, won a bursary to the ELC Art and Craft Centre in 1980 and now teaches at the Nyanga Art Centre.

headmaster who did not postpone examinations was Rex Pennington, headmaster at Soweto's premier private school, Pace Commercial College. In the harsh world of township politics this decision bestowed the image of sell-outs on his pupils and they had to run a daily gauntlet to get to school.

In the face of school boycotts the authorities have invariably reacted by closing down schools. Ever since 1955, when primary schoolchildren organized a boycott of their school in Dinokana Township near Zeerust, the state has responded by withdrawing educational rights, since the schools offered a ready-made forum for the exchange of political and cultural ideas and a context for direct action. Thirty years after the Freedom Charter of 1955, the Soweto Parents Crisis Committee (SPCC) organized a National consultative conference to discuss a situation in which teaching and learning had virtually ceased. This conference succeeded in bringing together representatives from black consciousness organizations, such as the Azanian People's Organization (AZAPO), and from the United Democratic Front (UDF). Differences were put aside in an effort to resolve the crisis in education brought about by pupils' refusal to put up with the 'poison' of Bantu Education any longer.

Alternative schools may have been out of the question, but an alternative course content was not. It was with this in mind that the first National Consultative Conference adopted the slogan 'People's Education for People's Power' as its theme. The African National Congress (ANC) sent a message urging a return to school and this message was endorsed at a second conference early in 1986 which saw the creation of the National Education Crisis Committee (NECC). This conference in Chatsworth, Durban, reiterated the 'back to school' call and resolved to implement people's education programmes wherever possible. The 1985 student slogan, 'liberation before education', appeared now to have been a little over-hasty and was replaced with 'education for liberation'. This change signalled the shift in emphasis from a suspension of education in the midst of open warfare to a strategy of emancipatory education.

'Adequate shelter'
Township Life and Art

The phrase, 'adequate shelter', to describe the minimal accommodation provided in the townships was first used significantly in the 1950s in the context of various actions taken to reinforce white control of black movement and labour. We have already seen how the township artists are hemmed in by political and educational structures. Now, let us look at the townships themselves and their effect on the art discussed here.

In the middle decades of this century, black artists suffered on two fronts: either they accepted second-rank status in the galleries and swallowed the criticism that they were sell-outs, or they struggled to find an outlet for their work in the impoverished and far-flung townships. In the 1980s, this situation has not changed much. A gallery given over exclusively to the display of work by black artists exists in Johannesburg and other smaller outlets sell work in Cape Town, Stellenbosch and Durban. In addition, a new

generation of artists has succeeded in securing exhibition spaces in the townships. However, these township venues are tenuous, understaffed and usually required for other cultural events as well. Although many artists exhibit in the townships, few manage to sell any work there.

The townships are not simply working-class residential areas characterized by poor facilities and run-down buildings. The majority of townships are of fairly recent origin; they date from the mid-1950s and their principles of land-tenure are directly linked to the apartheid master plan

Chests made and sold at Mai Mai Compound, Johannesburg. Mai Mai Compound reportedly got its name from a corruption of the English expression, 'My, my'. A previous compound manager used to respond sympathetically to tales of misfortune with this expression. He also allowed women to sell food and traditional medicine in the compound. In the late 1980s, the stalls in the compound cater mainly to the needs of miners returning to the countryside after the expiry of their contracts.

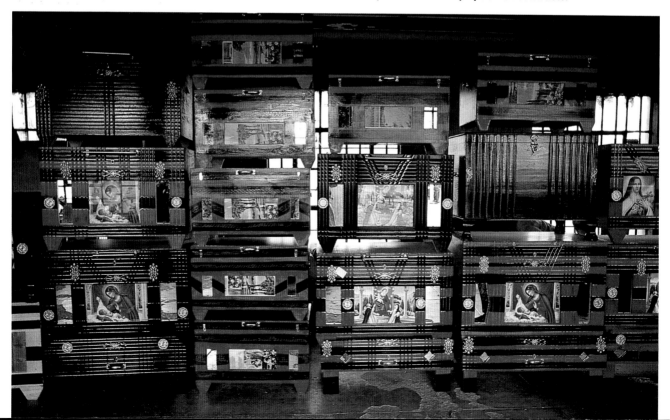

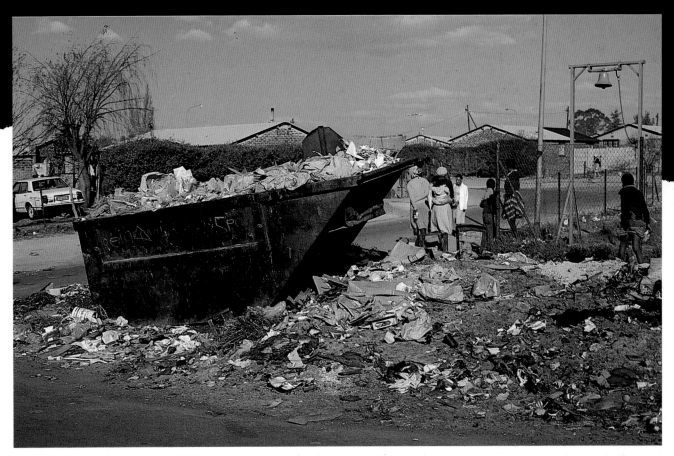

A street in Meadowlands, Soweto, 1985.

of generating separate National States for all of South Africa's African peoples. Although they are partly a response to the crisis in African housing, the townships are also part of a strategy to control African urbanization and thus the legitimacy of African demands for political rights. As such, their impact on artistic creativity is dramatic.

Firstly, the essential links with birth, fertility and renewal, so often the major themes of art, are disrupted by housing policies which were structured on the premise that Africans were temporary sojourners in the towns. Townships functioned as little more than labour reservoirs. The moral decrepitude of policies which admitted the bodies of 'work-seekers' into the towns, but neither their ideas nor families, has of course turned back on itself. Townships now resemble battle zones as young white army conscripts unwillingly undertake spells of 'township duty' against young black 'comrades'. The heroic themes of struggle against adversity do not compensate the artist for the agony of this war. Even the stench and deprivation do not outlast their passage into

paint or visual image. Like township jazz, township art is a celebration of a spirit which dwells elsewhere.

The second repercussion for artists does not awaken such antagonisms. Township life is far more communalized than ordinary city life and artists' subject matter is readily understood and shared by many people. Although visual art has not created the same mass audience as has music and urban performance culture, all the artists included in this book have experienced a high level of support from their immediate communities.

With the exception of some of the women artists, the artists discussed here have all lived for long periods in the townships. Conditions in the rural areas are so bad that men stream into the towns in search of work. Once there, they may not live elsewhere, even if they are in town for a short period. The central material fact facing the majority of South Africa's urban population is that by law they are forced to live in one of these segregated, impoverished and overcrowded townships situated on the periphery of 'white' towns and cities. This fact penetrates every aspect of urban life; and if we are to understand the art of the townships, we need to know more about this unique urban phenomenon.

In meeting the labour needs of industry and one of the world's richest and most advanced mining operations, care had to be taken not to put the security of whites at risk. The form and location of the townships went some way towards meeting this condition. In the mining organizations a unique 'compound system' was developed. Autonomous, self-enclosed, and policed by mine security officials, these compounds, like the Mai-Mai compound under Johannesburg's southern freeway system, have survived into the 1980s. These compounds affected the form of future townships. Like the compounds, the latter, too, were easily isolated and generally placed at some distance from the town centre. This isolation can be said to reflect the National Party's ideology of racial separation, but it is only when this crude formulation is taken further to embrace the need for a *docile* and *unorganized* work force that many of the special characteristics of the townships make any sense.

Before the boom of township developments in the 1950s, the Secretary for Native Affairs, Dr Eiselin, commented (NHPC Report, 1950, quoted in *Working Papers in South African Studies*, vol. 3, ed. Hindson, Ravan, Johannesburg, 1983) on their role in maintaining control over African lives: 'Only by the provision of adequate shelter in properly planned Native townships can full control over urban Natives be regained, because only then will it be possible to eliminate the surplus Natives who do not seek or find an honest living in the cities.'

Cyclist, charcoal on paper, Mboyi Moshidi, 1987. Mboyi Moshidi studied watercolour for two years under Dumisani Mabaso at the FUNDA Centre in Soweto. He now assists Tony Nkotsi in the printmaking section of the Johannesburg Art Foundation.

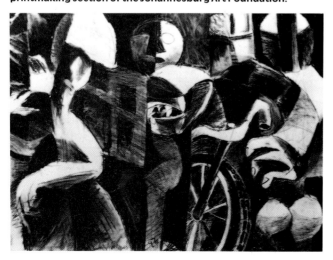

However, the Nationalists were not the only white governing party whose urban policies sought to control the presence of Africans in the urban areas. The first attempt to systematize African urbanization was made in 1923. Under the provisions of the Natives (Urban Areas) Act, employers were obliged to register all service contracts and influx was pegged at the levels required by industry. By 1937, whites had become sufficiently insecure to pass legislation which prevented blacks from purchasing land outside proclaimed townships. Eleven years later, the 'swart gevaar' (Afrikaans for 'black menace') policies, and the perception that the present level of controls over urbanization were insufficient to ease the severe shortage of farm labour swept the Nationalist Party into power in 1948. This party lost no time in making influx controls nationally applicable and so rigidly controlled that people without 'Section 10 rights' (a variety of qualifications based on birth, kinship and employment) could not remain in any town or city for more than seventy-two hours at a stretch. These Section 10 rights were soon to become infamous as thousands of people were prosecuted and evicted from the towns under this provision. So well-known did they become, that those qualifying for these rights described themselves as 'section tenners'.

These measures were policed through the 'pass' system and hundreds of thousands of arrests and 'endorsements out' were made annually. Four million pass related convictions were made between 1951 and 1962, and nearly 500,000 people were endorsed out of white towns between 1956 and 1962. Nationwide resentment towards these measures consolidated itself into resistance through the Defiance Campaign and the Women's Campaign. The Defiance Campaign was aimed at clogging the gaols by deliberately breaking pass and other apartheid laws. Begun on 26 June 1952, this campaign reached its peak during September when 2,500 resisters were arrested. However, the government reacted sharply by passing the Public Safety Act and the Criminal Law Amendment Act which imposed a three-year sentence on any person found guilty of breaking a law in order to protest against that law. In many cases, this sentence was harsher than that laid down for the original infringement.

But townships are more complex than their rows of sub-standard bungalows suggest. Not only are they a mechanism of labour supply, but their physical layout and administration is designed to absorb and displace discontent along manageable lines. Although the townships are a response to the crisis in African housing they are also meant to be a 'planned' and 'scientific' solution to political and economic problems. The 'planned' nature of this response is evident from the proposals submitted in 1931 for the design of

Orlando Township on a portion of the Klipspruit Farm which lay to the south-west of Johannesburg. Orlando is now part of Soweto, which despite its 'African' sounding name is simply an acronym for South Western Township.

These early proposals by prominent South African architects provided the physical framework and ideological justification for the wave of township development which occurred in the 1950s. Characterized by low rise, low density housing grouped around a regular grid of internal roads and separated from the urban centre by a wide buffer-strip, these designs bear a superficial similarity to the 'Garden City' concept advanced by European and American planners. The 'scientific' groundwork was laid down by the National Building Research Institute which published a booklet entitled *Minimum Standards of Accommodation for Non-Europeans*, which laid down the specification of the standard Soweto house, officially known as a Type NE 51/6 and 51/9. This type of house had an asbestos roof, no ceilings, three earth-floored bedrooms and an inside bathroom; the whole house measured a mere 28 by 21 feet.

The costs of establishing the townships were partially met by employers through the Native Services Levy Act. Under this act employers in the eighteen major towns were obliged to pay a weekly levy for each of their male employees. Pass fees, Labour Bureaux registration fees and beer hall profits were all important sources of additional revenue for the newly created regional Township Administration Boards.

These 'boards' granted themselves a monopoly over the running of beer halls and after 1952, when 'European' liquor was allowed to be sold in the townships, they extended their monopoly to cover these liquor outlets as well. Life in the municipal townships is still highly regulated. Even the brewing of traditional *sorgham* beer is banned to protect the profits made by the 'official' beer halls.

In spite of a chronic shortage in African housing, new township development was at the expense of the old. In this way older townships which enjoyed freehold rights were replaced by ones which did not. After Sophiatown was demolished in 1960, the land was sold to white working-class families and the authorities had the gall to name the new township 'Triomf' (Afrikaans for 'triumph'). Before its destruction Sophiatown was the cultural centre of a vibrant class of Africans who had urbanized but not Westernized. As the first of the so-called Western Area townships, Sophiatown had set the pace in the fields of music and writing, and its freehold title had led many African leaders to set up home along its untarred roads. In the days before the organization was banned, the president of the African National Congress, Dr A.B. Xuma, made his home there and the Odin Cinema was home to many of South Africa's

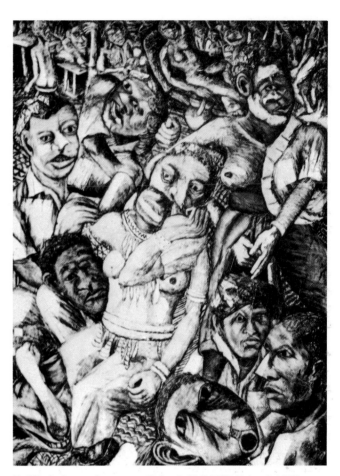

Untitled, charcoal on paper, Helen Sebidi, 1985. Helen Sebidi is primarily a potter and has exhibited with members of the Katlehong Art Centre where she also teaches. She is now studying art through the Johannesburg Art Foundation.

greatest jazz musicians. Despite its lack of services, its crude houses built of the poorest materials, its squalor and the violence of its *shebeens,* Sophiatown became a symbol of intellectual and political militancy.

The removals from Sophiatown and other Western Areas townships, which began in 1955, were the experimental forerunners of a policy which sought to site as much new African housing in adjacent 'homelands' as possible. Despite resistance and rent boycotts, these removals have continued until the present time because ethnic separation is the cornerstone of apartheid. One result of this policy is a bizarre situation where some of the townships which serve the capital city of Pretoria are more than a hundred miles away in KwaNdebele, an area which appears likely to become South Africa's next 'independent' National State. The men and women who sleep on the four-hour bus ride home every night must reflect on the fact that, in one way or another,

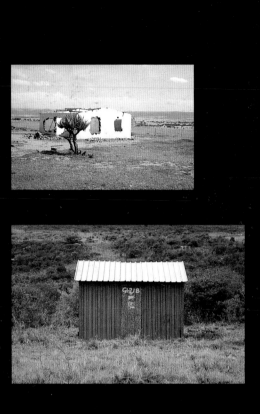

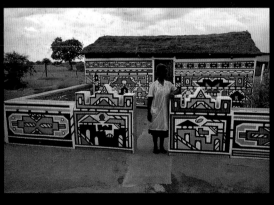

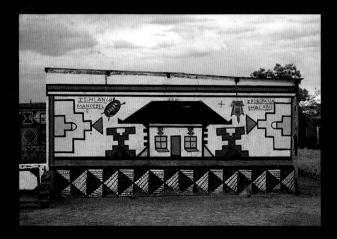

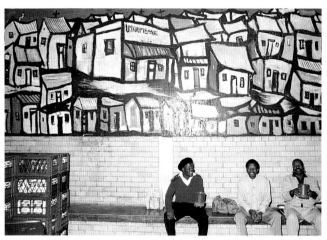

Above: *Umkhumbane*, enamel and acrylic on primed cement plaster, George Msimang. This mural was painted on the wall of a beer hall in Umlazi Township outside Durban in 1978. A rare example of official patronage, this mural was one of ten commissions from the architect of the building and paid for by the Port Natal Harbour Authority. With its strong decorative elements, this mural offers the men who frequent the beer hall a poignant reminder of the old, mixed-race shanty town which was known as Umkhumbane to its Zulu residents and as Cato Manor to residents of Indian extraction. Indian market gardeners in the Cato Manor area had begun renting their land out to African families in the 1930s and, by the time it was demolished in 1952, Cato Manor was a sprawling and congested settlement. In the face of poor conditions and in defiance of the Natives (Urban Areas) Act of 1923, the growth of this squatter community was a desperate attempt to keep families together.

Left above: remains of house after people were removed from the area known as Ten Morgen, eastern Transvaal, 1987.

Left middle above: Government issue tin hut, Ntambanana Resettlement Area, Empangeni, Natal, 1984.

Left middle below: Sarah Mahlangu at her house, Mabhokho, household acrylic on cement plaster. Women are taught to paint by their mothers. Sarah Mahlangu helped her mother and appears to have borrowed some design elements from her. In this way popular elements like the *tshefana* motif and the stepped pattern are passed on from one artist to the next. The artist draws out her design in black outline directly on to the wall without any preparatory sketches. Afterwards, certain areas are filled in with colour. The white paint, which is made from slaked lime, gives the murals a startling clarity. Sarah says that the stairways and round-arched doorways of the buildings which flank her gateway are drawn from memories of Pretoria.

Left below: end wall mural at Maphodla, household acrylic and washing blue on cement plaster, Sophie Mguni. The artist has dealt with the problem posed by the distorted rectangle of an end wall by establishing a picture frame. Symmetry is highly regarded as an aesthetic element and the artist has placed her subject centrally within this border. Significantly, she has chosen to depict a non-traditional house. The artist has provided herself with *trompe-l'œil* equivalents to fabricated windows and electric lights.

Opposite: Mr and Mrs Masilo outside their house, Valspruit, 1985.

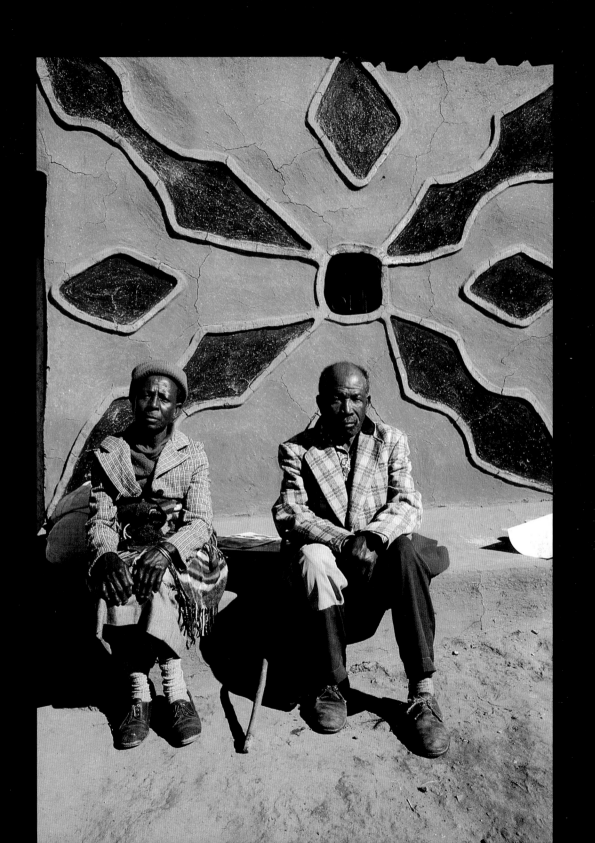

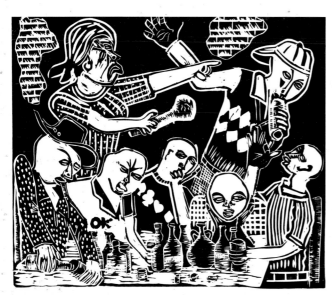

Shebeen, linoleum relief print, Tommy Motswai, 1982.

Quarry Worker, linoleum relief print, Robert Siwangaza, 1986.

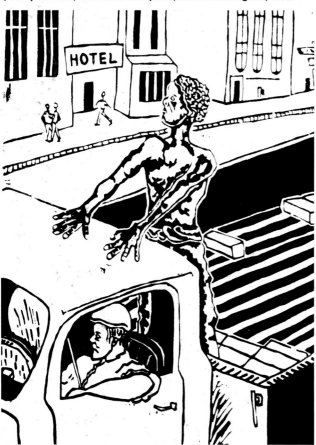

they have always been on the move. Displaced from what is now called KwaZulu/Natal in the sixteenth century they have been jostled by rivalries between the Manala and the Ndzundza clans; they lost their land after losing a war which was fought because their chief refused to pay taxes to the Boer Government; then they were removed from the Winterveld north of Pretoria after the Tswana homeland took independence in 1977. Now, finally, they have been bullied by Mbokotho vigilantes into accepting 'independence'. These vigilantes became active in 1985 at the time of the proposed incorporation of the Moutse area into KwaNdebele. Since that time they have maintained a wave of terror against opponents to the area of KwaNdebele taking independence. The area was declared a 'homeland' in 1972 and it became a 'self-governing' area in 1981.

The area of Cato Manor, which in the 1930s was a market gardening area owned by Indians, became in the late 1940s a major site of squatter resistance. Its closeness to Durban's centre meant that landowners could profit from shack rentals and by 1952 nearly ninety per cent of the population was African. In 1949, appalling conditions goaded the residents of Cato Manor, or Umkhumbane as the area was known, to march on the city centre during the Durban Riots.

It has been argued that the provision or withholding of housing is an important element in the South African Government's arsenal of political control over the African people. This is evident from the twofold response to township resistance. Firstly these 'riots' were savagely put down by the police, and secondly, African urbanization was outlawed under the Native (Urban Areas) Amendment Act of 1952. This act repealed the previously inefficient influx control system and passed the onus of its enforcement onto employers who would now be breaking the law if they employed an 'unregistered' work seeker. This act also provided for unrestricted powers of arrest over every African over the age of sixteen who was not in possession of a valid reference book.

In 1979, the Riekert Commission of Inquiry into Legislation Affecting the Utilisation of Manpower ushered in a number of reforms, the most important of which set aside the restriction on being in a 'prescribed area' for more than seventy-two hours. However, in the late 1980s, no African has an unqualified right to remain in an urban area or an unqualified right to live in an area of his or her choosing.

'Sharp!'

The Artists and their Art

Sharp!' is an exclamation of approval among South Africa's urban proletariat. American in origin, it is applied to anything which puts one over on 'whitey', or which offers a purchase in the slippery world of getting ahead. The towns are the centre of this world and the nature of the bus service between city centre and township has pushed Toyota into the number one spot among automobile manufacturers. Rows of minibus taxis, once declared illegal to protect bus company profits, have been christened 'Zola Budds' and now line the bus terminus kerb two deep. Disco music blasts out from record shops on to litter-strewn pavements rendered impassable by hawkers and seemingly untended lines of brown paper carriers. The sounds from these 'convenience' stores at the bridgehead between urban centres and the far-flung townships indicates the primacy of music in urban black culture.

Historically, music has not only been the focus of social and cultural life in many townships, but it has also been a site of resistance. Not only do some lyrics offer trenchant satire on state legislation, but in South Africa's polarized society even apolitical songs communicate a sense of cultural pride in black political consciousness. Although there are differences in the origin and the following of *ingoma ebusuku* and *marabi*, both music forms grew up in opposition to the hymnal music sanctioned by the African Eisteddfods. Both of these forms were also completely ignored by the record industry.

This industry was awakened to the promise of a large market for 'black' music after Reuben Caluza's recording success in England in 1930. Caluza himself was a noted ragtime performer and black American music exerted a significant influence on black South African culture. Spurred on by industry rumours that Aaron Lerole's hit *Tom Hawk* had netted Columbia Records a fortune in sales against a tiny one-off payment, a new spirit of belief in the predictions of local talent scouts sprang up and thousands of pressings were made and sold. Significantly, these sales were to black listeners. Since then, independent black producers such as Raschid Vally and groups like Philip Thabane's Malombo have achieved financial independence and considerable local and international acclaim.

The same degree of popular success has not been achieved by black visual artists. In the field of art, galleries and dealers are not organized into anything resembling an industry. Galleries are located in the city centres or affluent suburbs and cater to an exclusively white clientèle. While there is ready acceptance of the work of black artists, very few artists succeed in making a living from their art. Some artists have found jobs in related fields. Madi Phala and Sam Nhlengethwa have jobs as set designers in television. George Msimang works as an illustrator with the black press. Others teach. Andries Teklimane gets by doing pencil portraits of people in his community. Velile Soha teaches at the Nyanga Art Centre, tries to sell his serious work and paints seascapes for people in Nyanga.

A number of artists who have not had any art training appear to be doing better commercially than many who have. Koloane and Dhlomo think that this has something to do with buyers' preferences for works which appear naïve, since they are seen to be more 'African' and thus more authentic. As a result of the collapse of the subsistence base offered by the 'homelands', a number of people who had been migrant workers for long periods have entered the art market in an aggressive way. Mukhuba, Seoka and Maswanganyi found a way of turning the constant stream of motorists on their way to the game parks to their own advantage.

The most important difference between music and art can thus be found in the fact that contemporary black art did not find a black market. This has had repercussions, not only on the content of art done by black artists, but also on the style of that art. The curator of the FUBA Gallery, David Koloane, has complained that the art market has prevented artists from experimenting: 'The more naïve the artist, the more they want him to remain that way'. Cut off from their buyers by language and 'Group Areas' legislation, black artists have had scant chance of assessing how well their work is communicating. Communication, or lack of it, has become synonymous with sales figures alone. In turn, this has led to a perception among collectors that much black art is commercialized.

Consequently, when the work of a few artists who lived in the rural areas was first exhibited in Johannesburg in 1985 many believed that a new art form had been discovered. Quickly labelled 'transitional', this work not only looked modern but looked suitably African as well. In fact it was not new at all. It only appeared new in the context of an art market which insisted on its metropolitan primacy. However, much of this work was innovative and compelling by virtue of its conception and the authority with which it was executed. One would have to be extremely cynical to hold the artists responsible for the fact that the art market had quickly moderated its practical concerns about the presence of wood-borer and had opened its vaults to this work.

Phutuma Seoka

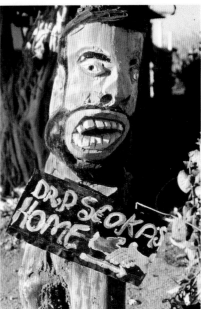

Carved signpost, enamel paint on wood,
Phutuma Seoka, no date.

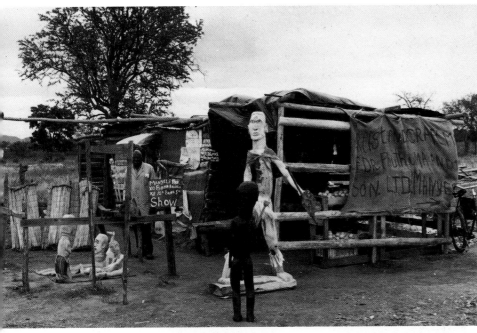

Seoka's studio and 'gallery',
c.1976.

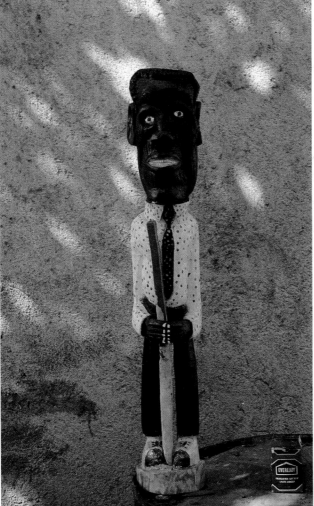

*Portrait of Madifukwane
Mohale*, enamel paint on wood,
Phutuma Seoka, 1985.

We are familiar with the image of men
walking barefoot, but this familiarity
has not prepared us for the reflection
of that image in the work of Phutuma
Seoka. Like other sculptors, and here
one thinks of work by Gabriel Kubhoni
and Philomon Sangweni, Seoka does
not depict the specific incident, but
chooses instead to give expression to
a communal experience.

By avoiding the usual subject-
matter of contemporary sculpture as
it is canonized in South Africa – that is,
forms in space – Seoka created a
'tourist art' that jolted the
establishment in South Africa and in
Europe. Although his figures,
thronging to a distant workplace, are
partly suggested by the natural forms
of velvet corkwood, they also flow
from his lived experience as a contract
worker. The most striking aspect of
these barefoot workers is not their city
clothes, but their confidence. This
confidence, which has been
painstakingly built up by the union
movement, is not confined to rallies
and the football stadiums. The inner
city areas, once the exclusive preserve
of white shoppers, have been
transformed by what traders like to
call the black market. Wages are low
but clothes are high on the list of
priorities. Two-tone Fleishmans and
genuine alligator Jarmens are a virtual

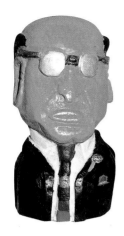

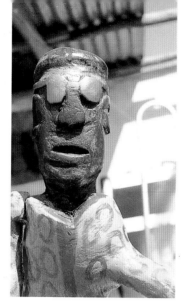

Left: *Man with Sunglasses*, enamel paint on wood, Phutuma Seoka, 1985.

Far left: *PW*, enamel paint on wood, Phutuma Seoka, 1986.

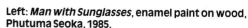

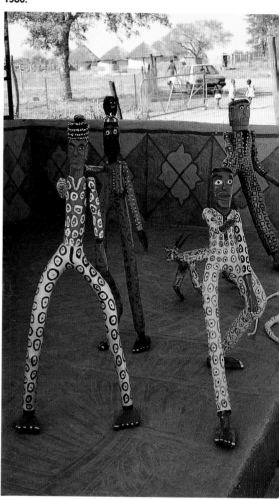

necessity for those urbanites who do have jobs. Thus, when Seoka accepted a portrait commission from Madifukwana Mohale, the headman of the village of Botsha-belo, he is presented in his town clothes. Seoka saw invested in this local dignitary all the power of a ruler: clean white shirt, two-tone shoes and a rifle between his knees.

Phutuma Seoka was born at Mojaji in the Lebowa area of the northern Transvaal where his father worked as a cow-hand. As a young man Seoka sought employment on the Reef and worked at various jobs until 1966 when he heard that his father had lost his job on the farm and been forced to move to Molototsi, a resettlement area in Lebowa. Seoka left his job and went to look after his father.

Why did he start making sculptures? Seoka says that the idea was suggested to him by a traditional doctor as a cure for a

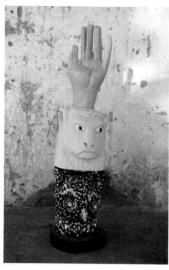

Hand/Lion/Owl, enamel paint on wood, Zacharia Seoka, 1987.

Figures at Molototsi, enamel paint on wood, Phutuma Seoka, 1985.

recurrent dream he had had about a large mountain snake. He dutifully carved an effigy of the snake and placed it under his bed. This early success led him to conflate physical and mental attributes and he carved a psychological self-portrait of a man with a snake on/in his head. Men possessed by the spirit of an elephant seemed to follow naturally and it was not long before Seoka had attracted wide critical attention.

Some of this attention has focused on his preparedness to copy himself and to engage assistants. By ignoring the established criteria of uniqueness, Seoka has imperilled his growing reputation, but has forged a new aesthetic. Zacharia, Phutuma's son, also produces exciting and compelling works such as the enigmatic *Hand/Lion/Owl*.

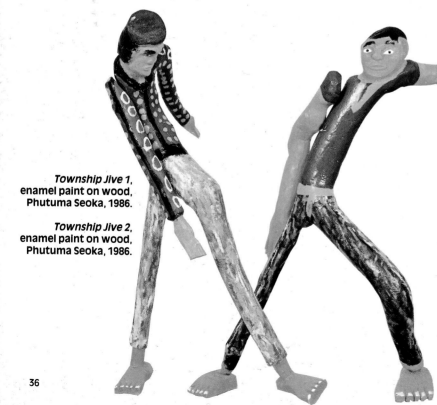

Township Jive 1, enamel paint on wood, Phutuma Seoka, 1986.

Township Jive 2, enamel paint on wood, Phutuma Seoka, 1986.

Right above: *Snake*, enamel paint on wood, Phutuma Seoka, 1985.
Right below: *Snake Dream* (detail), enamel paint on wood, Phutuma Seoka, 1985.
Opposite: *Township Walk*, enamel paint on wood, Phutuma Seoka, 1985.

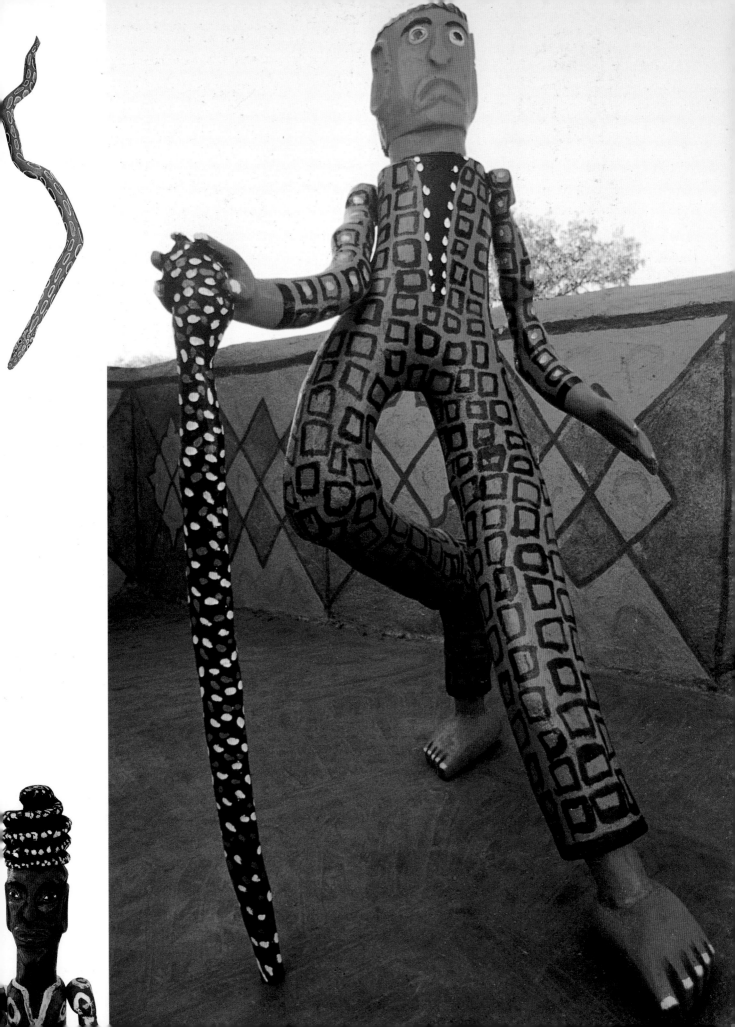

Noria Mabasa

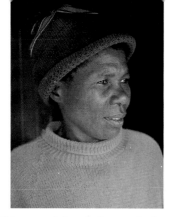

It has been said that traditional African sculpture is the symbolic terrain for the communal expression of something which is intractably personal. This formulation applies today, despite the fact that contemporary African society has been torn apart by political and economic forces. The residue of that symbolism and its effects for society can be seen in the work of Noria Mabasa.

Mabasa lives at Tshino village in the Vuwani area of Venda. The social organization of this village is given visual expression in the intricate lacings of hedges and low *lapa* walls which mark off private and public space. In Noria Mabasa's homestead the *lapa* walls are embellished with bas-relief sculpture and the entrance is flanked by male and female figures modelled in unfired clay. These figures do not fulfil a purely decorative function. They face inwards and give symbolic expression to the roles that courtyards, as social units of space, play in regulating social intercourse and maintaining social equilibrium.

Born in 1938, Noria Mabasa worked in the kitchen of a local farmer until the mid-1970s. Feeling insecure about the first small clay figures which she made, these were given away to local children. Today she pays an artist's tax to the local chief and digs her clay from river banks. Her naturalistic figures are coil-built and fired in an open straw fire. Although she has been offered the opportunity to become involved in a timber growing enterprise she prefers to make sculpture. Like Phutuma Seoka, she finds spiritual release in this activity and some relief from what she calls 'bad dreams'. In the eleven years that she has been producing sculpture she has steadfastly

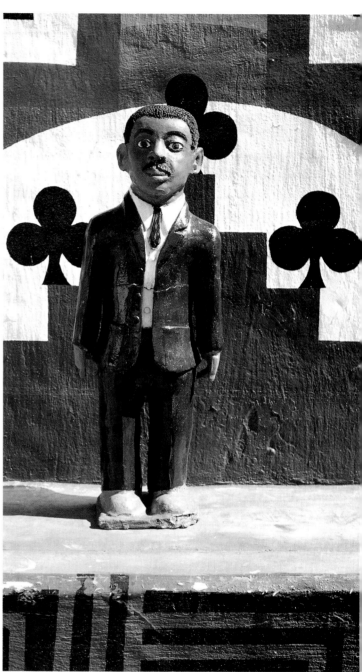

Venda Businessman, enamel paint on fired clay, Noria Mabasa, 1986.

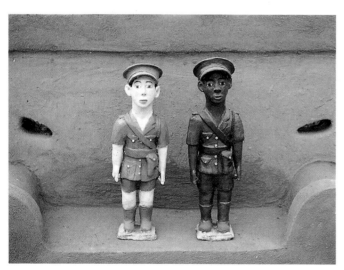

South African Policemen, enamel paint on fired clay, Noria Mabasa, 1987.

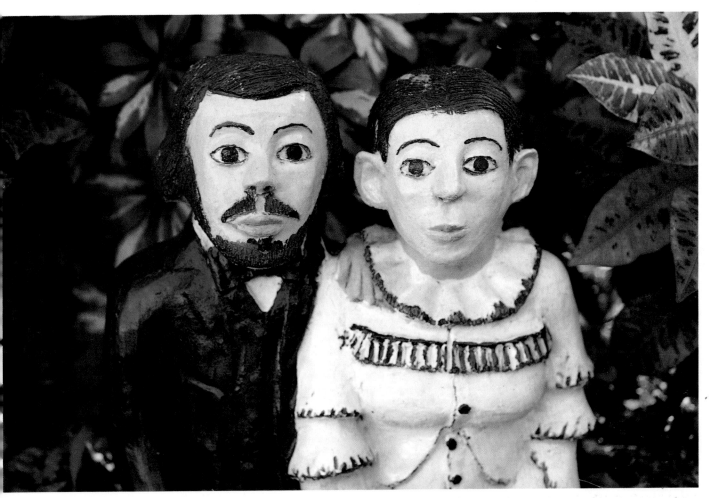

Colonial Couple (detail), enamel paint on fired clay, Noria Mabasa, 1987.

committed herself to exploring women's experience of life in the countryside during the long wait for the return of their husbands from the towns.

The story of contemporary black art is also a story of contact with Western influences. This has led to art becoming the site of a struggle for survival in a social environment which has always undervalued African social and religious values. Noria Mabasa has recently built a rectangular house with metal windows along one side of her courtyard. The house is 'modern' and reflects the financial independence that her contacts with art dealers have brought her. As has already been suggested, the art market is

a lot more robust than artists' egos or their bank balances. Sensing that 'colonial' figures would conform to foreign expectations of black art, a dealer (Lionel Finneran) gave her a copy of a page from a history of clothing styles and an order for a number of such figures.

It is difficult to work out who is patronizing whom in this situation and Mabasa has continued to produce enigmatic figures which she repeats over and over again, often to the irritation of collectors. Her pastiche of a baby-faced South African policeman is a sly piece of flattery. Asked about her intentions in making this piece, she lifted her shoulders and said, 'They are the protectors of the white people'. In the

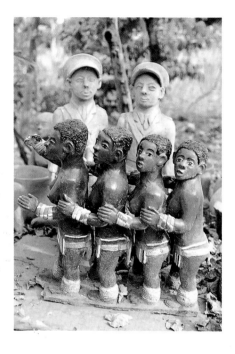

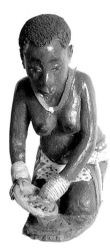

same way that a photograph of an armed police vehicle in a protest poster may achieve a liberatory as opposed to a placatory effect, so too her ubiquitous policemen have made their way into the homes of people who actively oppose apartheid.

The bourgeois concept of the work of art as a unique object, wrested from the tortured imagination of the lonely artist, has no application to either Seoka or Mabasa. Seoka has said, 'When you sit under a tree, you feel cool. When I sit under a tree, I feel hot because I look up and see money! There is a snake. There is a baboon.' Both artists reject the status of sculpture as a unique object. Since their work sells for the price of a print, few people will blame them.

Far left: *Domba Dance*, studio view, enamel paint on fired clay, Noria Mabasa, 1987.

Left: *Woman Washing Dishes*, enamel paint on fired clay, Noria Mabasa, 1985.

Left below: *Woman Feeding Child*, enamel paint on fired clay, Noria Mabasa, 1985.

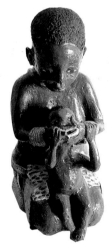

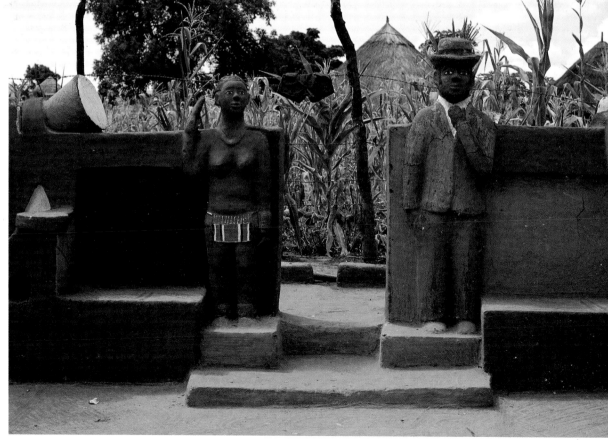

Mabasa Household at Tshino, Venda, sun-baked clay, Noria Mabasa, 1987.

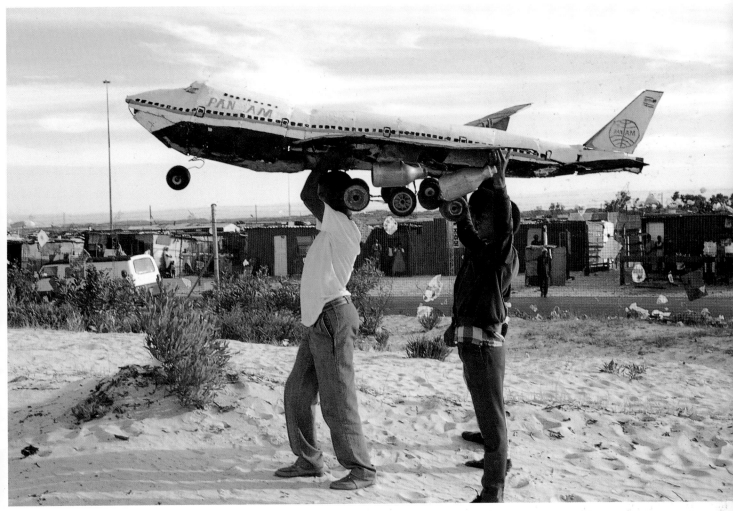

Pan Am 747, painted tin, wire and found objects, Titus Moteyane, *c*.1983.

If one takes the time, copperplate calligraphy can be achieved using a cheap ball-point pen. In a note describing his early interest in making things, Titus Moteyane achieves this effect by laboriously thickening the vertical stroke of every letter. He writes that his mother gave him the nickname, 'Handjievol' ('handfull'), because he was so adventurous. He is not at all complicated about his reasons for making buses, aeroplanes and trains out of old cans and he writes that he would like to be 'a million year'. Unfortunately, this is not likely unless he starts charging more than very modest sums indeed for his Pan Am Boeing 747s.

Moteyane was born in the Pretoria township of Atteridgeville in 1963. He finished school in the townships and teamed up with Joseph Chauke to form a band. Chauke sings in a deep jazz voice, while Moteyane imitates the sound of bass guitar and trumpet. Together, they have appeared on television. Indeed evidence of a multi-talented handyman is present in everything he attempts, and there is more than a trace of the shaman in his recreation of fleets of vehicles to go with his buildings, houses and dams. Asked where he gets the inspiration for his work, he replied significantly: 'By going on top of mountain and looking'. However, his cars and trucks are also derived from a close observation of form and shape; it is not only the Mercedes three-pointed star which identifies one model as a Merc and the next as a Rover. He also envisages the founding of a World Art Museum with representative examples of planes and trucks from every manufacturer.

Moteyane has not studied 'art' and has not picked up its mannerisms nor has he understood its mechanisms of approval. His first patrons were his school friends, and his singular skill in procuring and working scrap metal led to his work being sought out by collectors. This market for 'folk art' has grown but he no longer has the inner resources to remain a child and he has stopped making things.

Johannes Maswanganyi

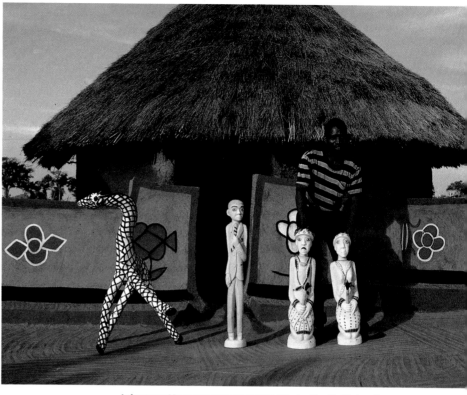

Johannes Maswanganyi outside his studio, Noblehoek.

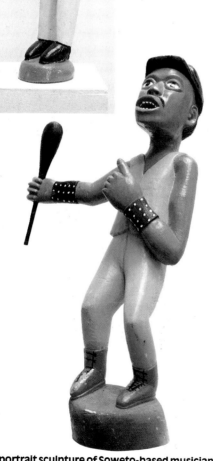

Above: portrait sculpture of Soweto-based musician, Paul Ndlovu, enamel paint on wood, Johannes Maswanganyi, 1987.

Above top: *Rich Man*, enamel paint on wood, Johannes Maswanganyi, 1987.

It is a common error to believe that people who have not been to an art school have not had any art training. Johannes Maswanganyi, like many others, learnt how to carve from his father. The art of carving *jsuri* for grinding maize is under threat of extinction from the availability of commercially ground 'mielie' meal and the Maswanganyi family was a poor one. The demand for these vital household items, as well as wooden spoons and bowls was not great in the village of Msengi, and Maswanganyi travelled as far as Tzaneen in the north and Soweto in the south to sell his wares.

His figure carvings brought him critical attention and a solo exhibition at the Market Gallery in Johannesburg. His carving of the popular recording star, Paul Ndlovu, is typical of the new urban character of his work. Drawing freely on the products, if not the aesthetic conventions, of industrial society, Maswanganyi's carvings have a surprising immediacy and confusing diversity about them. Carved figures of Christ, pop stars and animals do not appear to be bound by a single aesthetic purpose. What appears in some carvings as a superficial catoptric gloss, akin to the 'gloss' of the enamel paint he applies so freely, is sometimes tellingly incisive. His *Rich Man* is a curious amalgam of obsequiousness and authority. When one considers the South African situation, these are exactly the qualities a black businessman needs to succeed in adversity.

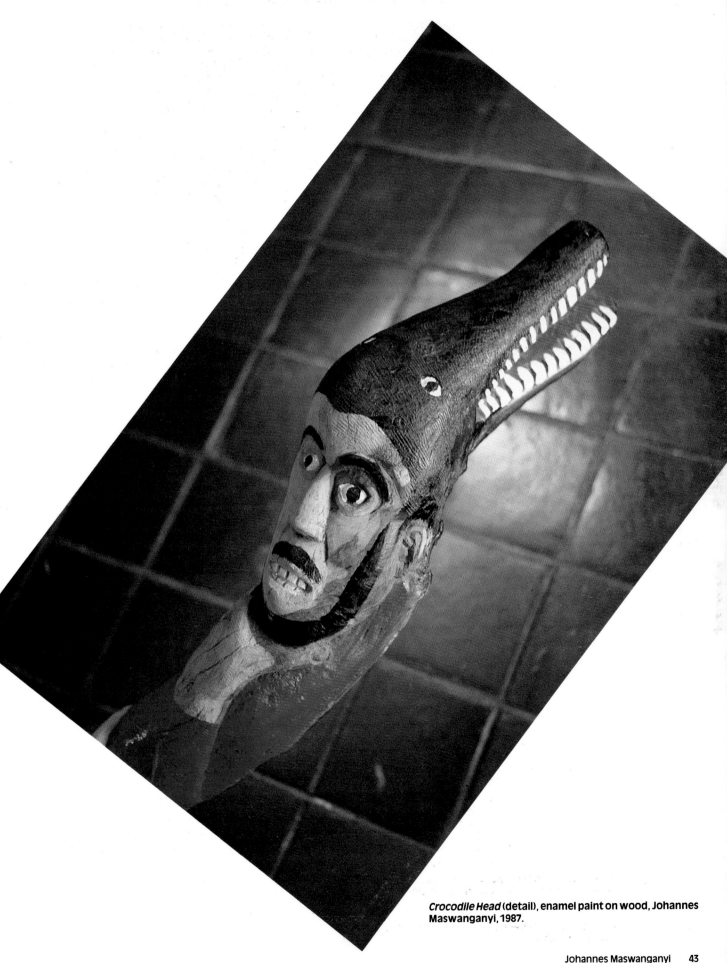

Crocodile Head (detail), enamel paint on wood, Johannes Maswanganyi, 1987.

Tito Zungu

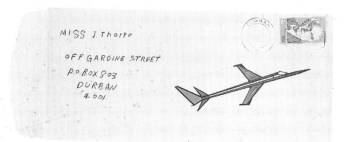

Envelope, ball-point pen ink on envelope, Tito Zungu, 1975.

The work of Tito Zungu presents a paradox. As is common with children born to dispossessed parents in the late 1940s, there was no family land left to plough and when he was about fourteen years old (he is not sure of his birth date) he took a job on a farm near Stanger. Later he got a job working in a dairy in Pinetown, a suburban area of Durban. His early childhood and his first work experiences were thus intimately bound up with the earth and with things that grow in it, yet the first drawings he made as an adult were of multi-storeyed boats, aeroplanes and buildings. The paradox is deepened by the fact that he never went to school and never learnt to read or write.

A clue to the understanding of this phenomenon can be found in the unique form of his art. Tito Zungu's first drawings, and indeed the greater volume of his work, was done in ink with a ball-point pen on ordinary envelopes which he sold to his work mates for less than the price of a picture postcard; these envelopes were used to send letters back to wives and children in the countryside. They served as postcards in the sense that they gave the recipient a visual picture of where the sender was. His decorated envelopes found a market, not in spite of their unreality, but precisely because they offered migrant workers a way of transcending the hardship of city life and a way of impressing family members living in the countryside.

By focusing on the pageant of city life, its crisp improbable colour and delightful lack of depth, Tito Zungu has created an illusory world in which we can all believe. His fantasy world has a double allure. On the one hand, it has the sophisticated allure of big buildings, jets and ocean liners. On the other, his world has an engaging innocence, one which renders redundant all social and political issues.

Not understanding the meaning of letters, in *Jet Set* Zungu has thought that the abbreviation '(PTY) Ltd' is the name of a large corporation with ubiquitous interests in most other companies. Not only are all the envelopes done in the early seventies marked *'Made in South Africa (PTY) Ltd'*, but we also find *'Worlds Most Experienced Machine (PTY) Ltd'* and *'Jet by Air Mail (PTY) Ltd'*.

Durban's assortment of buildings have become mosaic palaces complete with minarets and cantilevered eaves. Incredibly, each brick, each storey has been ruled in with a ball-point pen. Sometimes the colour has been built up

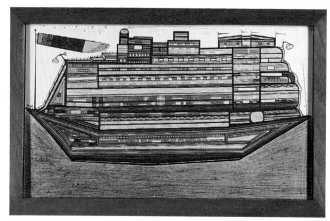

Ocean Liner, ball-point pen ink on paper, Tito Zungu, *c.*1974.

through overlap, a process Zungu calls 'twice and twice'. The drawing called *1972*, like other similar ones, conveys an overall impression of opulence. The clocks may not keep time, but the building is so big that many roadways are necessary to service it. A profusion of windows and catwalks make up the façade, while corbelled towers give rise to distant vistas of untold splendour and, need one say, wealth. Strangely, although we see a small flowering shrub in the foreground of this drawing, we do not see any people. There is no sign of life in any of the windows. Even the drawings of aeroplanes clearly show the pilot's window and yet the pilot and crew are not visible in any of them.

Zungu's wife also works for the Dominican Sisters and his humble and self-effacing attitudes are typically pious: 'I have liked to look for 15 or 14 years at the white man's houses and things like aeroplanes and ships; I don't want them, but I do get jealous about these things, I don't know what to do about them.' His work initially enjoyed working-class support from his friends and colleagues on the basis of the perceived needs of their situation. This relevance was not forged from the actuality of their day-to-day working lives, but from the

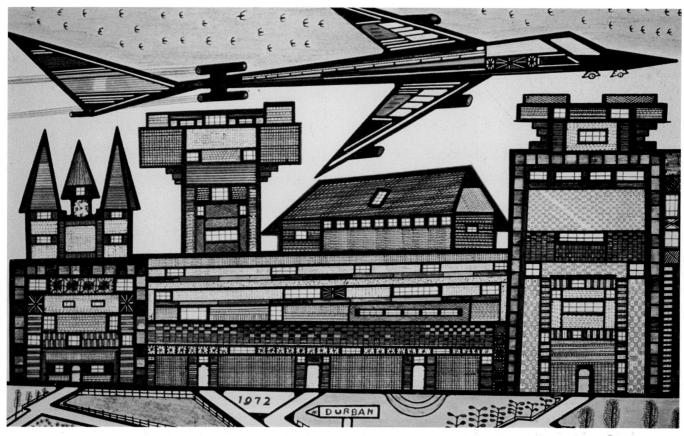

1972, ball-point pen ink on paper, Tito Zungu, 1972.

fact of their separation from loved ones. In a curious but surpassingly human way, his glorification of city life provided his work mates with a way of coping with life in the ghetto.

For white buyers, his work provides a way of coping with life in the main house. His delightful zany creations seem to show that life in the backyard ghettos cannot be all that bad. Somehow, the evidence that one person has been able to rise above the material conditions of his own exploitation, washes away the contrary evidence of those who grumble and complain. Since 1971, when he won a prize in the Art SA Today exhibition, he has not lacked white buyers for his work.

There is now a waiting list for his work. Dealers have stepped in and he may not sell from his 'studio'; they decide who may buy and who may not. But Tito Zungu does not want to take the step of becoming a full-time artist. He has consistently stressed the point that he cannot work unless he is in the right mood. His work is very taxing on the eyes and it takes him weeks to finish a single drawing. There is no doubt that he could produce more work if he gave up his job as a cook but, for the time being, this is something he does not want to do.

'In 1970 I sold an envelope to one of my African friends in Westville who in turn showed it to his employer. She was very impressed and asked me to visit her. She then referred me to her friend Miss Thorpe from the South African Institute of Race Relations. I showed Miss Thorpe a few examples of my work which she bought. She has since bought many more of my drawings. I have been awarded the prize of R180 for some of my work and have sold some for about R110. It is through her that I have gained publicity and have become known to interested people both overseas and back here in South Africa. As you will have noticed, my talent has developed slowly, and I hope with God's help to go on improving. I am deeply grateful to Him for His help.'

Nelson Mukhuba

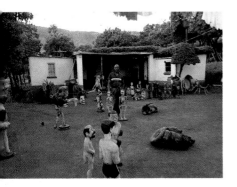

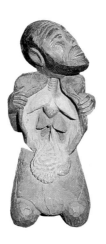

Nelson Mukhuba at his house, Tshakhuma, Venda.

Nelson Mukhuba's fame as an artist was no measure for his violence as a man and in February 1987 he destroyed his whole world. Soon after returning from a visit to Johannesburg where he was the guest of honour at an art exhibition he chopped down his fruit trees in preparation for a ritual purging which left his wife and two of his daughters dead. He then wired up the windows of his house before pouring petrol over his 'museum' and himself. When the flames became unbearable he crawled out of a window and hanged himself from a tree.

Mukhuba's work hints at the presence of the tragic and psychopathic. One of his carvings depicts a man literally tearing open his chest, not so much in anguish, as in desperate pride. In a way, it is a

Left: *Self Portrait*, enamel paint, stainers on wood, Nelson Mukhuba.

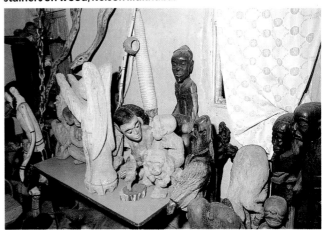

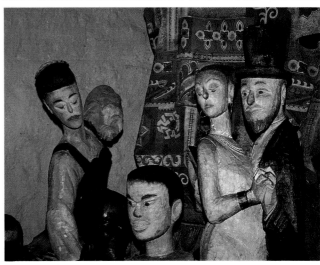

Above: views of Nelson Mukhuba's storeroom, 1984.

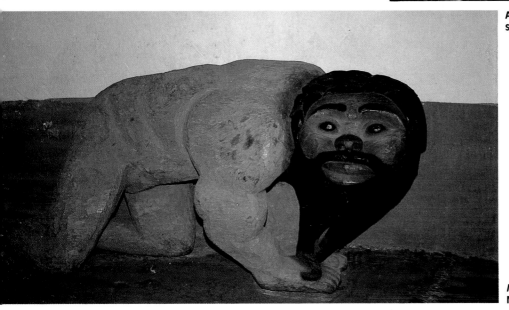

Nebuchadnezzar, enamel paint on wood, Nelson Mukhuba, c.1979.

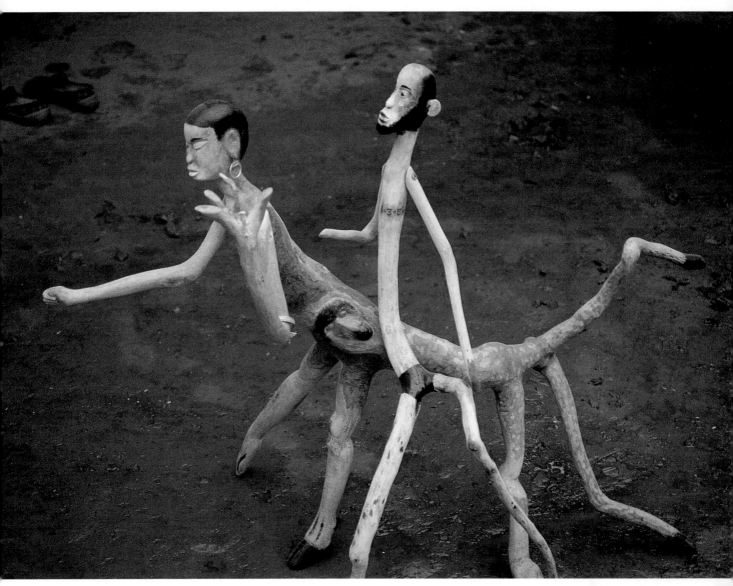

Dancing Figures, enamel paint on wood, wire nails, found objects, Nelson Mukhuba, 1984.

shocking presentiment of the agony of a man who has lived through two adolescences: once biologically, and once emotionally as an old man starting a new career. Of this apparent self-portrait he says: 'That picture (here he points to the sculpture) with his chest open, with his heart, lungs, everything open shows you that I am an artist that can see inside the wood . . . I can see the picture while the wood is still on the tree. I am the doctor of wood because I can see inside the wood. By carving, I make people see my talent, see that I can see inside the wood, to see the figure and the shape of the sculpture.'

In the late fifties, as a stage electrician's 'boy', Nelson Mukhuba watched from the wings as the Shadows and other famous groups performed in the whites-only theatres of Johannesburg. He vividly remembers the Colosseum and the Empire Theatres. But, unlike hundreds of other aspirants, he actually went on to form his own band, Nelson and the Phiri Boys, and to record with groups such as the Zoutpansberg

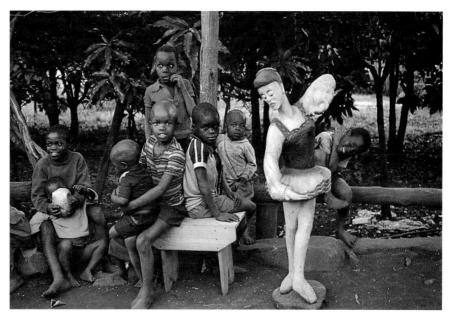

Ballerina, enamel paint on wood, Nelson Mukhuba, *c*.1974.

Merry Makers. At the time he was working successively as a carpenter, welder, gardener or house painter. He even tried his hand at upholstery. Finding jobs more difficult to come by as he grew older, he was thrown back on the symbolic terrain of his own VhaVenda culture. Drawing on this reservoir of wood-carving skills he started carving drums for *domba* and other traditional ceremonies. He also succeeded in selling a few small carvings of animals on the roadside, and in 1980 his work was promoted by the Venda homeland on its stand at the Rand Agricultural Show at Milner Park in Johannesburg. The mediating agency of these homeland structures also led to his work being used, albeit unacknowledged, on Venda postal stamps. The rush to acquire an African veneer was not confined to the homeland authorities and Sun International Hotels used Mukhuba's work as free décor in their casino until he retrieved it in a rage.

After the BMW Tributaries exhibition in 1985 he achieved a marked degree of critical acclaim and his work is represented in most major institutional collections in South Africa. His visitor's book has entries from all around the world and a visit to his home in Tshakhuma was always made into a special occasion by his gifted wife and other dancers who made up the dance group Mahlombe a Muthandabinyuka. Mukhuba used to take part on stilts which he had carved to resemble the legs of a giraffe.

Realizing that the psychic income of their European tradition was dead, art students were leaving their art schools and travelling to be with Mukhuba. His prices rocketed tenfold. Success seemed swift in the slowness of time in Tshakhuma. The blast on the kudo horn which signalled the arrival of visitors was heard more often. Sensing the fickleness of success, the man who had previously been told by 'big people with good money' that his work looked like 'Bushman art', could no longer cope. He had sold his best pieces and he was too tired to make more. The man who struggled to find praise for the work of other artists could finally no longer find praise for his own.

Zamokwakhe Gumede

Gumede has said that the impulse for his work springs from two sources: his own life experiences and reflections on the nature of good and evil; more specifically, whether 'the devil still has a hold' on him. In *The Dice Players*, these moral questions are smothered by the strong anecdotal qualities of the tableaux. The evils, or merits, of gambling, somehow fail to strike home as real issues and the viewer is left marvelling at the technical control of the carving and the camaraderie of the players.

Gumede was born in 1955 and was imprisoned in the Oliviershoek gaol during what he calls a tribal war. His first drawings were scratched onto the wall of the prison. In 1980 he took a carpentry course at Mariannhill Monastery; however, his father had prophecied that he would become an artist, and he kept in touch with Smart Gumede and other artists who exhibited at the African Art Centre. In 1986, he submitted a piece to the Festival of African Art and won first prize. Since then he has been commissioned to produce work for the Catholic Church at Verulam.

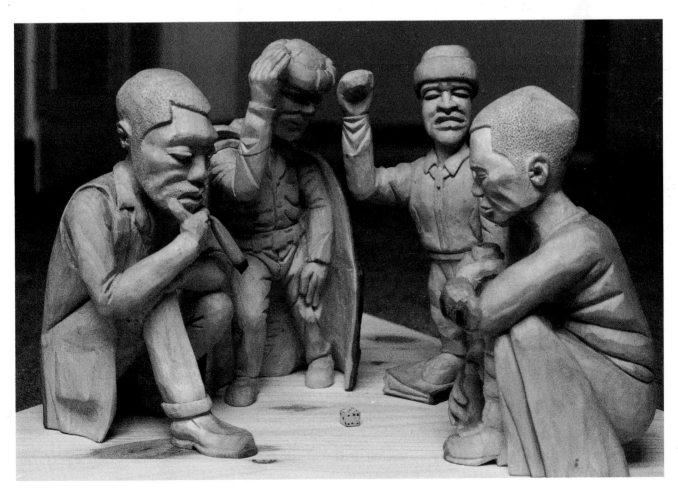

Dice Players, carved wood, Zamokwakhe Gumede, 1987.

Tommy Motswai

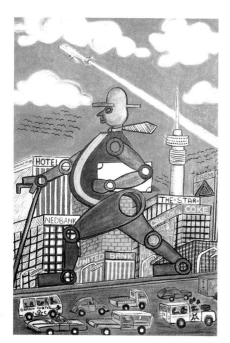

Citizen, oil pastel on paper, Tommy Motswai, 1987.

Tommy Motswai relies on his observations of incidental detail when making his bitter-sweet comments on urban life. In *The Tea-party* his victims are a smiling middle-class couple who are being entertained in an excruciatingly average South African home. Whilst the image of the aproned maid bringing in the milk may be somewhat passé, white South African viewers should squirm with embarrassment at the accuracy of his jaundiced colour scheme and telling choice of paintings. In his recreation of white suburbia, Motswai has bitingly signed one of the paintings within a painting with his own name.

His descriptions of urban experience are at times merely prosaic. His *Bus Stop* is just that. Spurning distortion or other dramatic devices he has catalogued various 'types' of person. In *Choir*, the lens of his sly wit ridicules damp-faced

Below: *Bus Stop*, oil pastel on paper, Tommy Motswai, 1987.

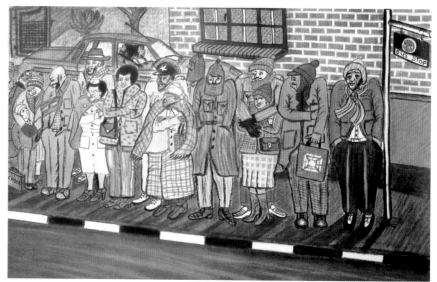

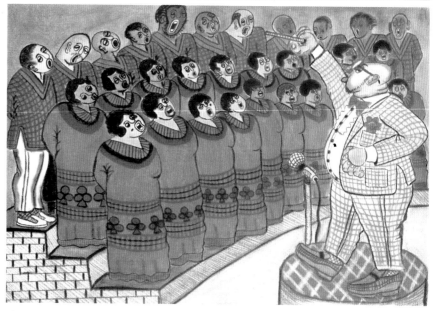

Choir, oil pastel on paper, Tommy Motswai, 1987.

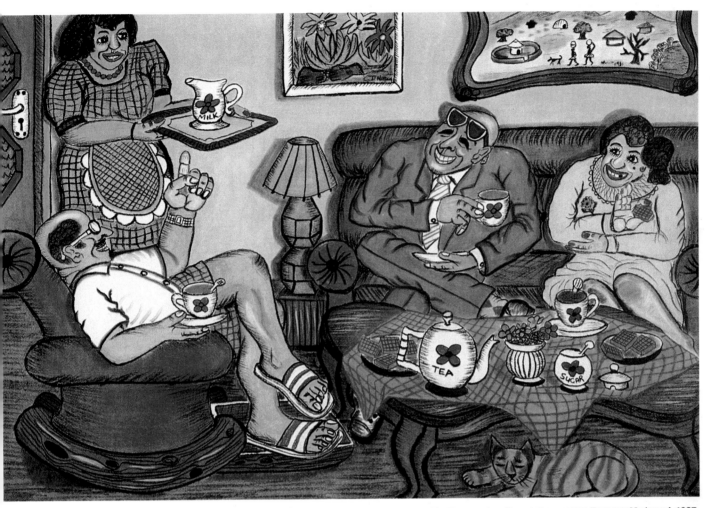

The Tea-party, oil pastel on paper, Tommy Motswai, 1987.

choirmasters and probes the pretentions of choir competitions. These events, relics of attempts to 'raise standards', live on in the sound stages of the SABC's Sotho and Xhosa services.

Tommy Motswai was born in Rockville, Soweto, in 1963. He was born deaf and completed nine years of school at the Kutlwanong School for the Deaf near Rustenburg. In 1983 he joined an art class at the Federated Union of Black Arts and in 1986 he won a study bursary in the Santam Children's Art Competition. Bearing in mind the lack of facilities for the deaf at this and other art schools, he regards himself as having been self-taught. In 1987 *The Tea-party* won a merit prize in the Volkskas Ateljee Awards.

Derrick Nxumalo

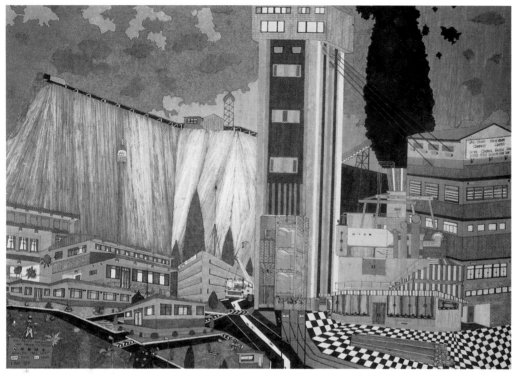

Vaal Reefs Exp & Mining Company Limited, felt-tip pen ink on paper,
Derrick Nxumalo, 1987.

Derrick Nxumalo also makes unpopulated landscapes and also came to critical attention through the efforts of Terry-Anne Stevenson and Jo Thorpe of the African Art Centre in Durban. In 1987 he was encouraged to submit one of his felt-tip pen drawings to the University of Zululand's annual festival of African art and won first prize.

His drawing *Vaal Reefs Exp & Mining Company Limited* represents, in kaleidoscopic fashion, the shaft-head environment of the mine. Not yet trusting his hand, Nxumalo makes use of a ruler to delineate his delight in the technological complexity of his working environment. His primary aim is to record and nothing escapes his dispassionate eye. From the wire-mesh on the office windows to the yellow arrows on the tarmac, everything is given equal, garish attention.

Nxumalo worked as a waiter and gardener before taking a contract with the Vaal Reefs Mining Company at Orkney in 1986. His keen eye has picked up the mine's safety record emblazoned on the company sign, '1,000,000 fatality free shifts'. This exercise in personnel relations is important and signals management's real concern over the safety of their employees in the shafts of some of the world's deepest gold mines. Historically, mines with reputations of being hazardous struggled to get workers willing to go underground. The Vaal Reefs mine has been struck by three disasters since 1980 which have claimed lives. The most recent of these, in January 1988, resulted in the death of six miners of the night shift.

Drakensberg Mountain is a model-train enthusiast's dream in which highways, under- and over-passes, streams, lakes, peaks and traffic signs just succeed in not colliding. As is the case with the world of model trains, there do not appear to be any inhabitants in this the most ideal of all worlds. The City Liner glides along with its curtains neatly tied back and its roof-rack aerodynamically at the ready, but there are no passengers. His focus is on the rich countryside through which he travels by bus on his way from his home in the farming district of Dumisa, KwaZulu, to the mine in Orkney.

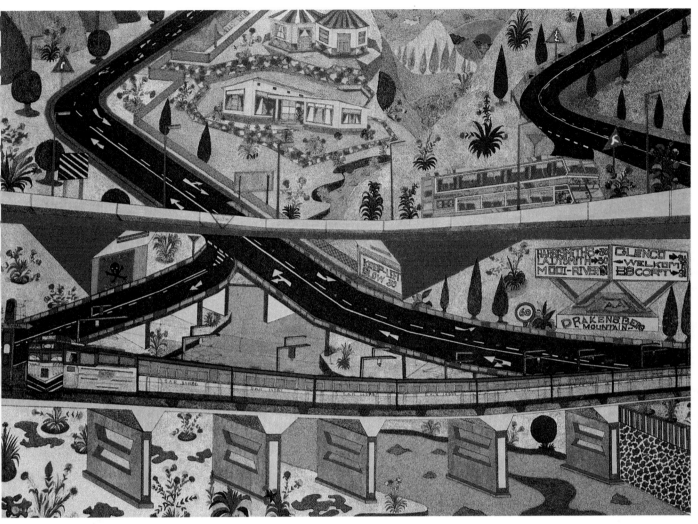

Drakensberg Mountain, felt-tip pen ink on paper, Derrick Nxumalo, 1987.

House painters

The provision of shelter is only the passive function of a house; its positive function lies in the degree to which it defines and protects the complex social relationships pertaining to people whose patterns of social organization are largely communal. In such a system, the divisions between private and public areas become very important.

Traditionally, these divisions were protected by the way individual households related to each other and by the strict codes of conduct which regulated social interaction. In this century, these divisions have largely been broken down by economic changes, although the house, as a social unit of space, still falls under the jurisdiction of the woman. Courtyards used to be an integral part of the household, set off from the public domain of the village by a low wall. Traditionally this was the area where visitors were received and it was the only part of the complex of thatched buildings into which men, other than husbands, were allowed. Consequently, the courtyard was thought to be an area of 'heat' or potential disquiet in the otherwise ordered whole of a woman's domain. Often it was only the walls which face onto the courtyard which received attention from the artists. Research by Catherine Vogel (*The Traditional Mural Art of the Pedi of Sekhukhuneland*, MA dissertation, University of the Witwatersrand, 1983) indicates that these walls were painted because the act of applying a suspension of earth pigments to the wall was considered to have a 'cooling' or beneficial effect. This 'cooling' effect was present, not only in the ritualized activity of painting, but also in the contemplation of its final effect.

Today, the art of wall painting is no longer confined to the inward looking walls of these courtyards and the pigments used are no longer dug from the soil; even the

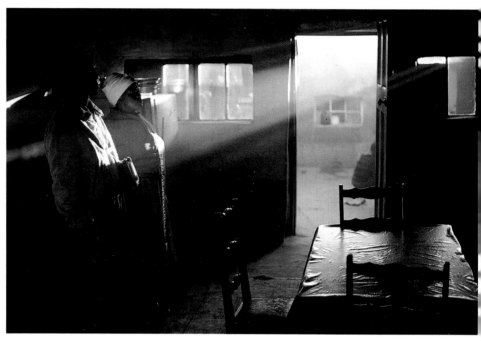

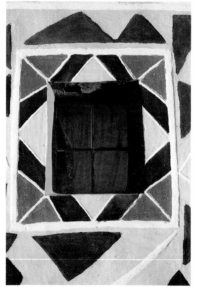

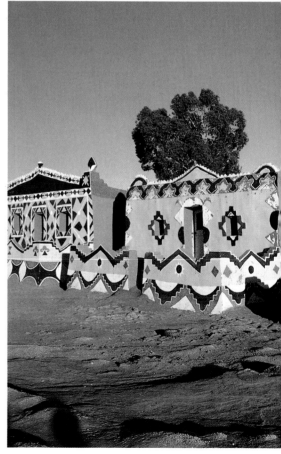

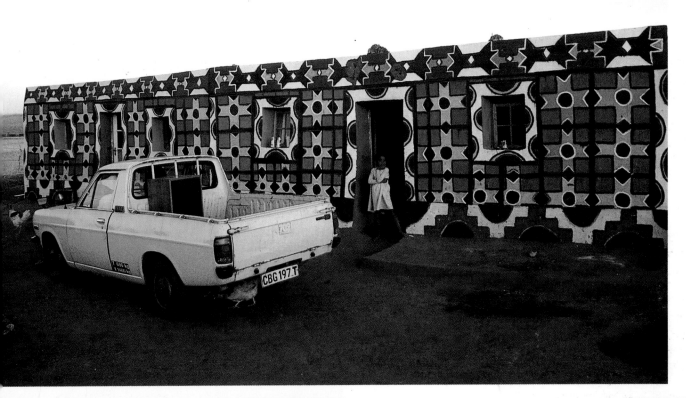

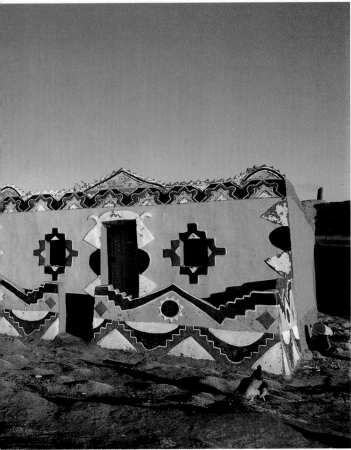

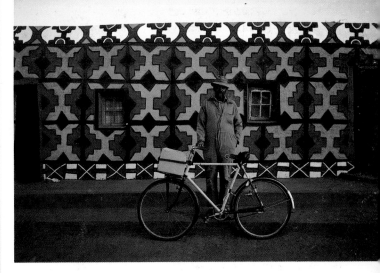

Opposite above: Michael and Emily Motsoeneng, Prospect Farm, 1985.

Opposite left: window detail, farmworkers' homes on Prospect Farm, Bethlehem, powdercolour, flour and milk binder, Emily Motsoeneng, photographed 1985.

Left: farmworkers' houses on Prospect Farm, Bethlehem, powder colour, flour and milk binder, Emily Motsoeneng, photographed 1985.

Above and top: farmworker's house on Klipskeur Farm, photographed 1985.

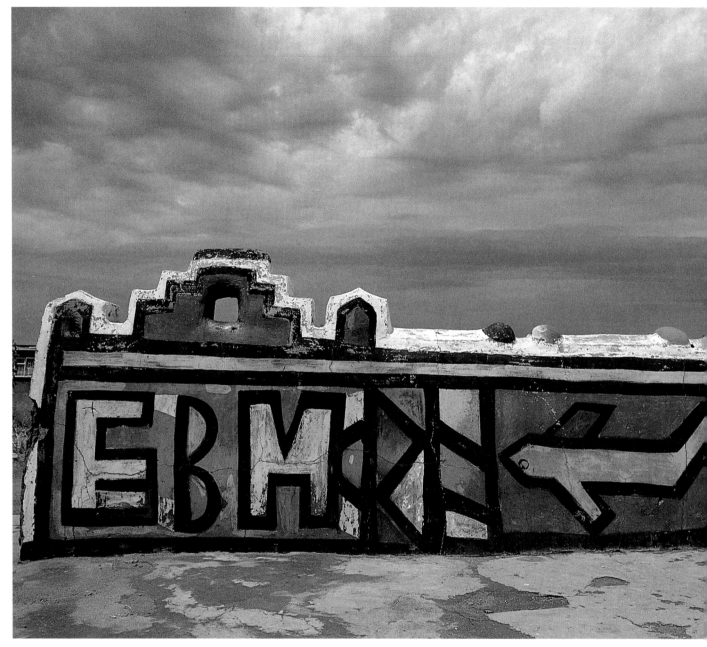

Courtyard murals at Weltevreden, KwaNdebele, household acrylic on mud and cattle-dung plaster, Marta Mahlangu, photographed 1987. The Weltevreden farm was bought in 1923 by Paramount Chief Mayisha with money raised for that purpose from his followers. Prior to that time, but after the disastrous rebellion against hut taxes, which resulted in the confiscation of all land belonging to Ndzundza, the people had paid rent for the farm.

activity itself is on the decline as political factors force more and more people into smaller areas of land and as women are drawn into the waged labour market. AmaNdebele house painting may appear to be the exception, but many people fail to make a distinction between the old, monochromatic designs (which do not show up on old photographs) and the more recent murals painted in modern acrylic polymers. Studies of wall painting among the Southern Ndebele people support the idea that regional styles exist (for instance, Elizabeth Ann Schneider, *Paint, Pride and Politics: Aesthetic*

and Meaning in Transvaal Ndebele Wall Art, doctorate thesis, University of the Witwatersrand, 1986) and there is clear evidence that official patronage after 1953, when the government promoted tours to a 'Ndebele Village', led to a more general acceptance of modern paints among the Ndzundza clan. Manala's and Sekhukhune's followers, however, continue to use oxides: red ochre, which facilitates communication with the spirits of the ancestors; white, which is anathema to malevolent spirits and thus applied to window surrounds as a kind of burglar guard for the soul.

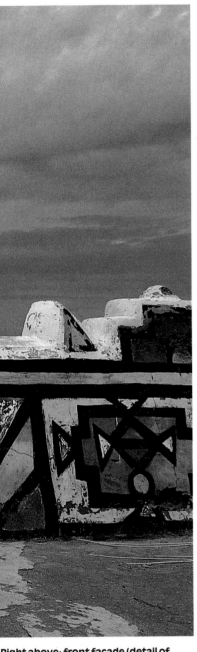

Blue, the colour of the sky and air spirits, continues to be obtained from washing blue.

Gender differentiation is common throughout Africa and is associated with many aspects of domestic and political life. Although aspects of the symbolic function of house painting have fallen away through contact with Christianity, the central symbolic connection with the house as a metaphor for continuity remains. Significantly, men are not invited to involve themselves in house painting. These murals express the world from a woman's point of view; at one level they appear to be almost geometric, at another they synthesize plant forms and patterns derived from woven grasses. Subject matter is not canonical; stepped forms are borrowed from razor blades and tree-like forms are derived from telephone poles. Emily Motsoeneng, who is seventy years old, has no need for black outlines and works directly onto the wall with her bare hands.

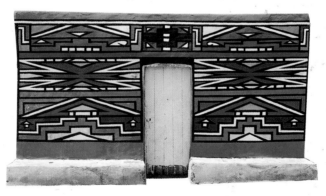

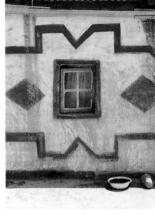

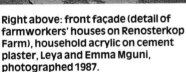

Right above: front façade (detail of farmworkers' houses on Renosterkop Farm), household acrylic on cement plaster, Leya and Emma Mguni, photographed 1987.

Far right above: rear wall (detail of farmworkers' cottages on Renosterkop Farm), oxide on mud plaster, Leya Mguni, photographed 1987.

Right: Julia Malaka and Melita Molokwane at Mountain Hill, photographed 1987.

Far right: houses at Mountain Hill, Venda, earth oxides and acrylic paint on mud plaster, Julia Malaka and Melita Molokwane, photographed 1987.

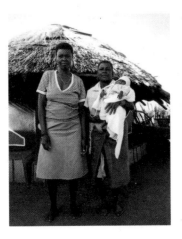

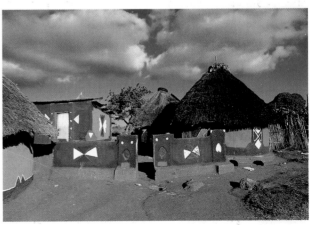

Artists and the struggle

The reform initiatives which were mounted in the field of education during the late 1970s were, perhaps not unnaturally, oriented towards the acquisition of commercial and technical skills. The question of art training was left unanswered and the few art centres which did exist struggled on as they always had.

However, developments in student politics led black artists to expect more from these centres than training in technique and theology. The most important development was occasioned by the walkout of black delegates from the 1968 National Union of South African Students (NUSAS) annual congress in Durban. The late Steve Biko, who at that time was a medical student at the University of Natal's Medical School, stated that black grievances could not be addressed in a non-racial organization in which blacks were the minority. Although black students supported NUSAS as a *national* union, Biko believed that a separate organization was needed to address legitimate grievances. Consequently the South African Students Organization (SASO) was formed in December 1968 at a meeting held at the Mariannhill Institute and it was inaugurated the following year at the University of the North.

The philosophy of SASO, that blacks could strip off psychological feelings of inferiority by emphasizing black pride and dignity, was in no way comparable to government efforts to enforce separate 'cultural advancement'.

Visual artists, however, did not appear to measure up to the commitment evidenced by writers and dramatists and they had not yet produced work considered sufficiently relevant to warrant banning by the state. This perception led a group of artists to form the Organization of South African Artists (OOSAA), which in 1975 startled artists by sending out a 'Message to the Artists of South Africa'. This message was couched in melodramatic language and resulted in a few dozen replies from artists who were interested in 'Uniting by means of a manifesto, those South African artists and sympathizers who feel that the artist has a positive role to play in the realization of the true cultural potential of Africa'.

The minutes of the organization show that OOSAA did not succeed in attracting significant numbers of artists. After a year of seminar meetings and consultations with other cultural bodies it attracted more interest from the security police than it did from black artists and one of the initiators, Barry Gilder, fled into exile. In December 1975 the organization arranged a two-month lease on an old building in Mowbray for what was called 'The Workshop – Community Arts Project'. The realization among artists that they had the power to organize themselves was grasped sceptically, and the building of a genuinely representative South African culture seemed a very long way away.

On 1 May 1977, individuals from the Christian Institute, the South African Council of Higher Education, the Institute of Race Relations, the University of Cape Town and the Holy Cross Church in Nyanga were appointed trustees of the Community Arts Project (CAP). Over the years CAP has moved closer to labour and community organizations and now runs a number of out-reach programmes in the townships, offering classes in art, drama, dance and pottery. Artists and cultural workers who attended the 1982 Culture and Resistance Festival in Gaborone returned with fresh commitment which resulted in poster and T-shirt workshops being established under CAP's auspices. CAP now also offers a three-year, full-time art course.

During the ten years of its existence, the Community Arts Project has evolved to a point where its stated aim of providing an arts resource which was open to all at last appears to be realizable. Group Areas legislation makes cross-cultural contact almost impossible and these difficulties cannot be overcome simply by throwing one's doors open. Structures have to be built and alliances made which counter racial and class ideologies which have been in place for a long time. Although CAP struggles to survive financially, CAP will not accept money from local funding agencies such as the Urban Foundation because it is thought that this foundation is trying to strengthen the African middle class as a foil to progressive social change.

According to David Koloane, the Federated Union of Black Arts (FUBA) was established in 1980 in response to demands and needs as they were identified by artists, writers and dramatists at a meeting in Soweto in 1978. Under the general direction of Sipho Sepamla, FUBA offers training in music, dance, drama and fine art. Anthony Caro's visit to South Africa in 1981 prompted him to approach other internationally recognized artists to donate work to FUBA as a gesture of solidarity with oppressed artists in South Africa. The arrival of the FUBA Collection from England and the United States highlighted the need for exhibition and museum space. The FUBA Gallery was established in 1983 under the curatorship of David Koloane and offers artists an alternative exhibition space.

Artists are still struggling with the notions of accountability and democracy which other cultural and media workers have grappled with for some time. Once again, as in different cultures at different times, the individuality of the artist is at risk. In the wake of the Culture in Another South Africa (CASA) conference in Amsterdam, organizations inside South Africa are beginning to urge artists to forsake their non-aligned position and to enter the struggle. For many artists, both black and white, this is not a problem, as long as progressive principles are adhered to.

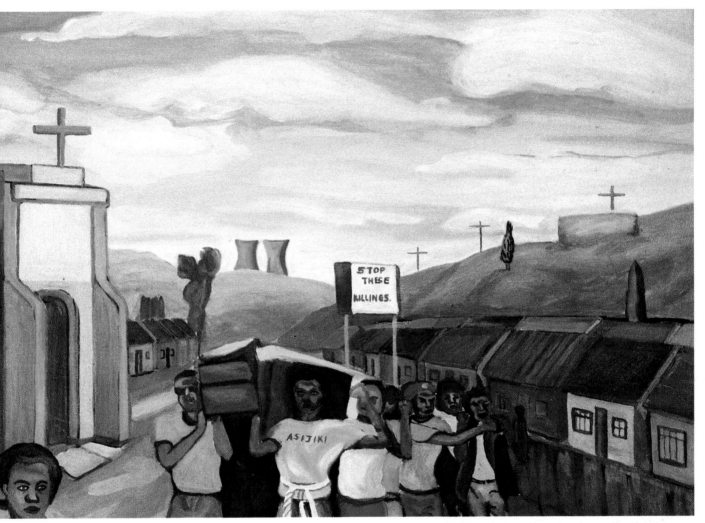

Asijiki-Stop These Killings, acrylic on board, Bernard M. Tshatsinde, 1985.

Johannes Phokela

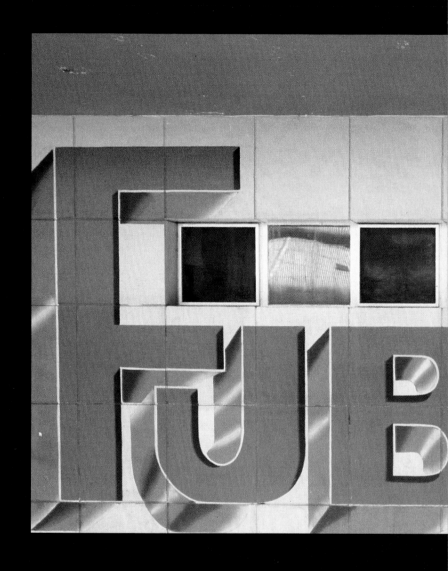

Federated Union of Black Arts
mural, acrylic on cement
plaster, Johannes Phokela, 1986.

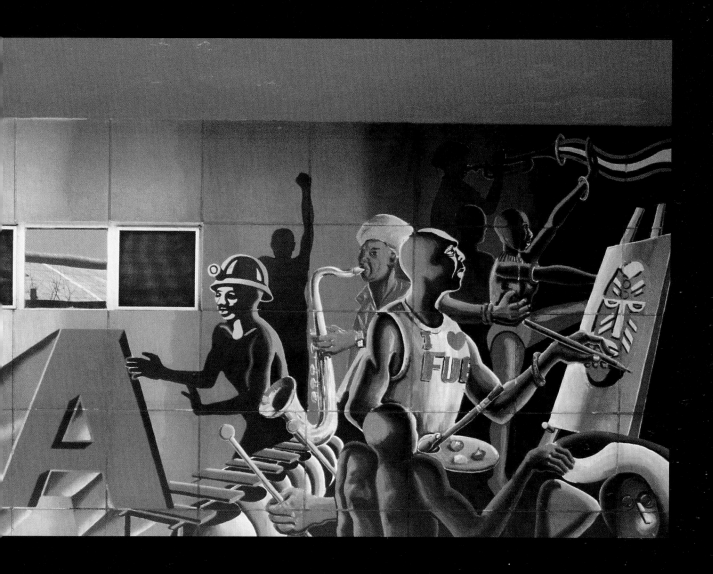

Billy Mandindi

Mandindi's series of relief prints offers viewers a cryptic reminder of Nongqawuse's apocalyptic prophecy that the sun would rise in the west and the white man would be driven into the sea if the Xhosa burned their crops and killed their cattle. In *Prophecy I*, the tragic consequences of this false prophecy are foretold in the prophet's own skeletal frame. Even her breasts, symbols of life and the nurturing of the Xhosa nation, are sadly made of bones. In another symbol of events foretold, the hand of a clock points to five minutes to twelve. Time is running out.

In *Prophecy 2* she is again full-blooded. The nation has regrouped and recovered its strength. The thought lines which emanated from her brow have now become the beams of a miner's torch, a symbol of servitude and migrant labour. Around her are depicted fragments of Xhosa resistance – a crop of spears and a hand grenade. A man is behind bars, the stairway leads nowhere.

Prophecy 3 is understandably not conclusive. The suggestion of a miner's lamp and helmet has been transmogrified into a calabash. What this image loses in subtlety it gains in precision. The once proud Xhosa farmers have been thoroughly proletarianized. Nongqawuse now carries a pick, but tellingly she also has a spear and shield hidden in her skirts. In an ambiguous double twist to the image, her one hand seems to be either holding back, or blessing, the young warrior who is carrying a grenade. For the artist, the day when the sun will rise in the west is still to come.

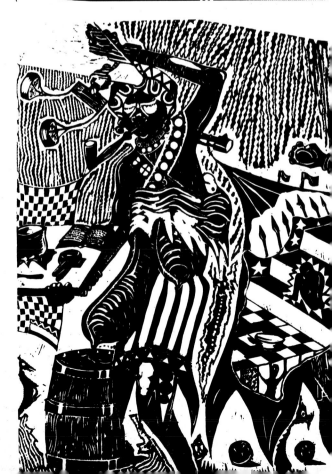

Right above: *Prophecy I*, linoleum relief print, Billy Mandindi, 1985.

Right: *Prophecy 2*, linoleum relief print, Billy Mandindi, 1985.

Opposite: *Prophecy 3*, linoleum relief print, Billy Mandindi, 1985.

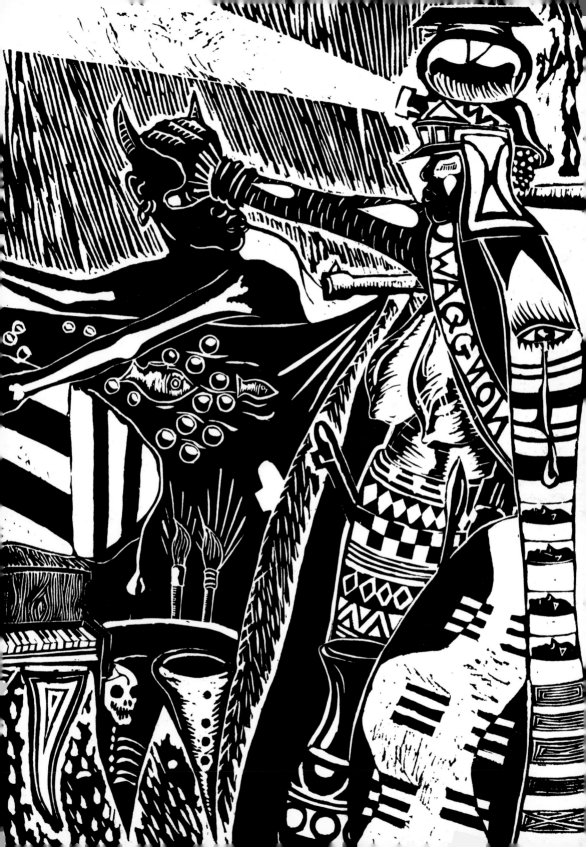

Mpolokeng Ramphomane

Mpolokeng Ramphomane's painting *For the Gift of Love* is typical of the more tutored and sophisticated technique of artists living within commuting distance of Johannesburg. Nearly two metres wide, it is large in comparison with the work of other artists to have graduated from the ELC Art and Craft Centre at Rorke's Drift. The nervous flick of brushstrokes in the background provides a bogus psychological space within which two lovers turn to face the viewer, their faces in sharp focus against a frieze of dark shadowy figures.

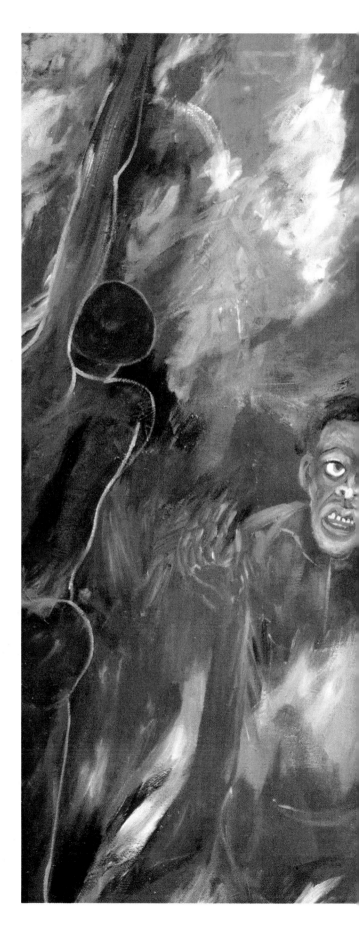

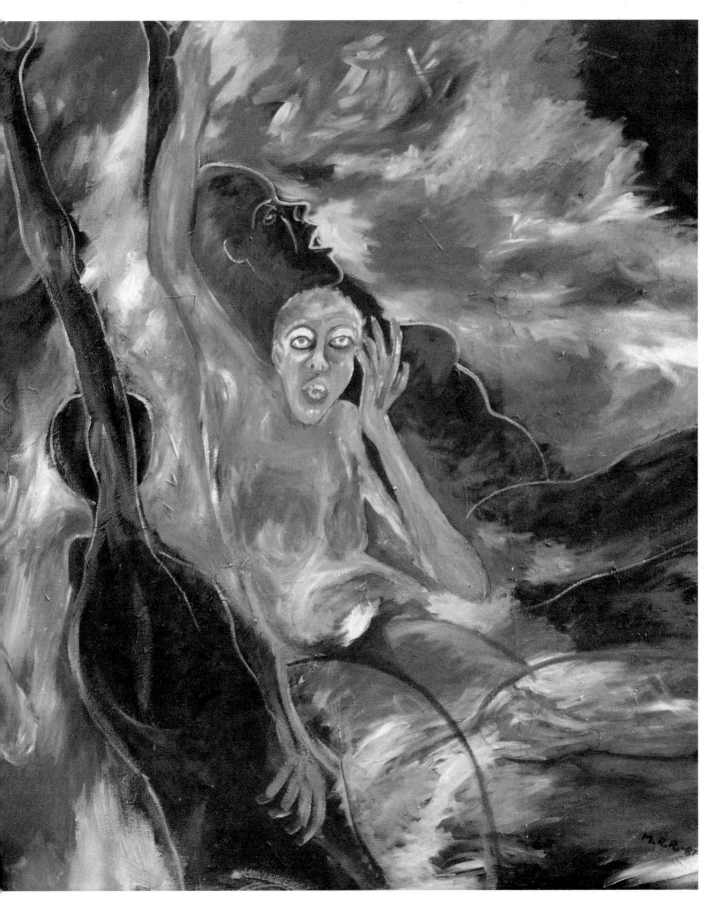

For the Gift of Love, oil on canvas, Mpolokeng Ramphomane, 1986.

Emile Maurice

Emile Maurice believes that art does not need justification. In a private interview he said, 'Art is a kind of truth which refers to social context. Politics is not a choice an artist makes about content – it is part of life's circumstances.' For Maurice, 'People's Culture' gives people access to cultural institutions. This way, he argues, 'people begin to see art as an expression of themselves as social beings having a culture'.

His drawing, *Music for Sebokeng*, intends to evoke contradictory sets of associations. In conveying complex meanings succinctly he has chosen an autobiographical approach. The seated woman is his aunt. This information would not be evident to the viewer, but the compassionate treatment of the figure goes beyond the normal device of caricature for the sake of ridicule. Both figure and violins appear to swim in the walled-off garden, borne along by the unheard melody and distant beat of far-off trouble.

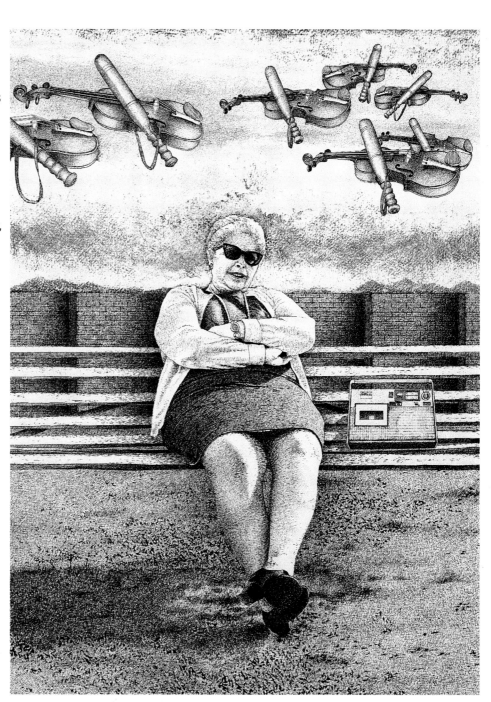

Music for Sebokeng, ink on paper, Emile Maurice, 1986.

Randy Hartzenberg

Under the direction of Francis Wilson, the Second Carnegie Inquiry into Poverty, held at the University of Cape Town in 1984, included submissions from community photographers, artists and film-makers. This etching was among those works of art which formed part of the conference proceedings. Hartzenberg, who has taught art at one of the leading 'coloured' schools in Cape Town for seventeen years, sees the conflict in South Africa as a threat to humankind as a whole. The shadow of the falling figure is a stain on what he calls 'our house', which he sees as a metaphor for the country as a whole. His image of massed storm clouds, rigid with advancing spears, carries as much a threat as a promise. The promise is well known, the threat is directed at the humanity of those who take the lives of others, for whatever reason.

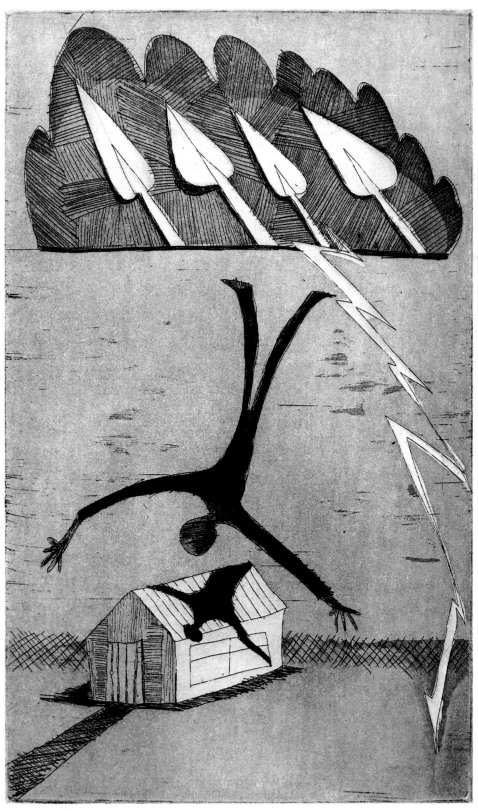

Untitled, etching, Randy Hartzenberg, 1984.

Craig Masters

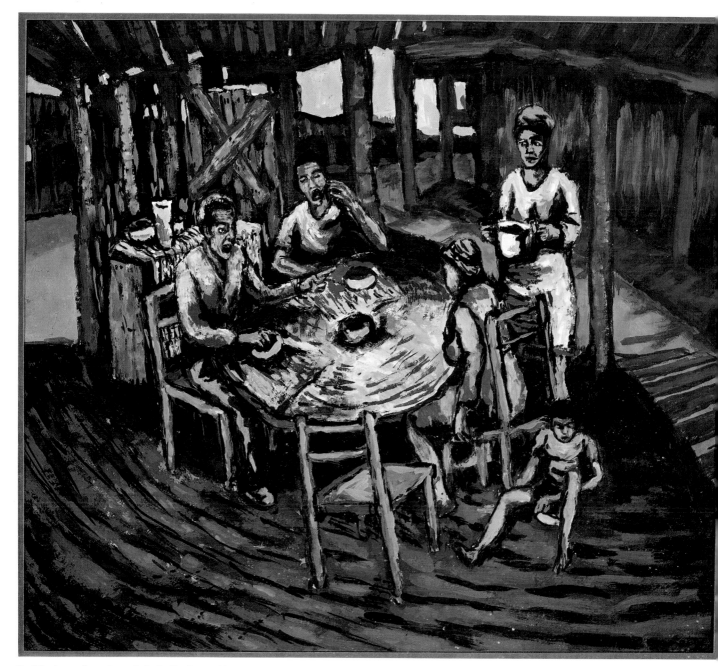

Untitled, acrylic on board, Craig Masters, 1984.

Luthando Lupuwana

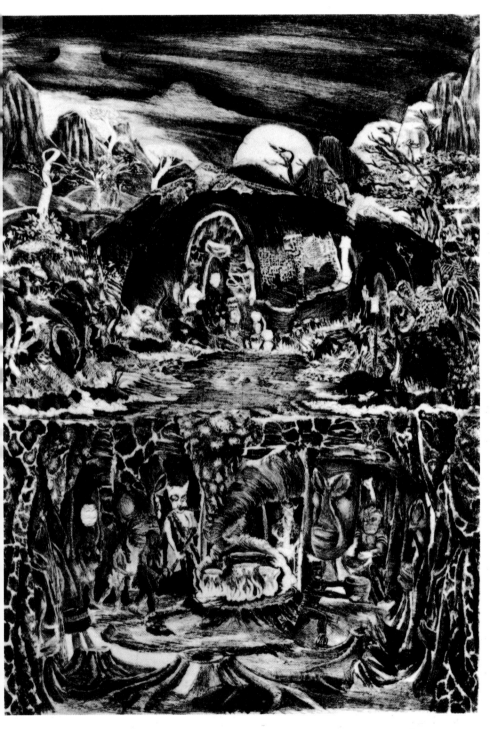

Luthando Lupuwana's *Renaissance* series of dry-point etchings were made while he was a postgraduate student at the Michaelis School of Fine Art, University of Cape Town. Like all his work, they are densely constructed and the viewer has to search the moonlit landscapes for recognizable elements with which to reconstruct the myths and legends of Africa. The Christian conception of the two worlds of heaven and hell is transposed into an African setting and given literal expression in *Renaissance 1*. Xhosa women descend into the underworld to refill the *iingqayi* which they carry on their heads from the large cauldrons which have been kept on the boil by the spirits of the ancestors.

Lupuwana admires the meticulous work of the Renaissance artists (whose work he first saw in 1979 as a student at the University of Fort Hare) and he believes that art's role is to make knowledge visible. The medium of dry-point is exacting and intolerant of the slightest slip, but Lupuwana says that it allows him to work anywhere since he does not need a large studio.

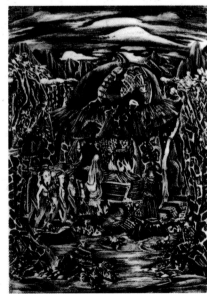

Above: *Renaissance I*, dry-point etching, Luthando Lupuwana, 1986.

Right: *Renaissance X*, dry-point etching, Luthando Lupuwana, 1986.

Madi Phala

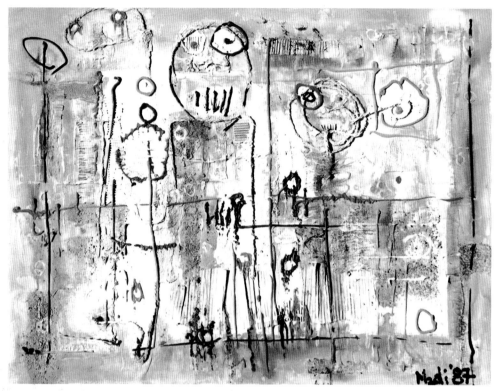

These Guys Are Heavy, mixed media on canvas, Madi Phala, 1987.

The debate as to whether 'black art' is primarily figurative or abstract has found a focus in the Thupelo Art Project. This project was launched in 1985 with funds from the United States – South Africa Leadership Exchange Programme (USSALEP). Since then it has offered places to about eighteen black students per year for a two-week workshop run by a visiting artist or critic. Thus far, Peter Bradley attended in 1985, Kenworth Moffett in 1986 and Graham Peacock in 1987.

Moffett's claim 'that a sophisticated, ambitious abstract art ... an art which is wholly life affirming' is emanating from the townships is exaggerated on two counts. Firstly, it is not emanating from 'townships', it is emanating from the Thupelo Workshop in the heart of a white farming district for two 'all expenses paid' weeks. Secondly, the connection between 'abstraction' and 'life-affirming' art is sententious. Most artists who have attended the workshop say that they have benefitted from their experience and some have changed their style of working quite dramatically. Some of these artists, among them Tyrone Appollis, argue that if the call for a form of social realism is ideologically inspired, so too is the call for an art which 'transcends' the specific relationships of existence.

No one wants to dictate to foreign artists who come to South Africa, but questions have been raised as to why Thupelo has always chosen abstractionists to run the workshops. This emphasis has seemed strange in the light of the international reassessment of figuration. At a time when artists such as Steven Campbell are leading the revival in regional painting with his 'Scottish' scenes and eclectic whimsy, it seems inappropriate that the formal remnants of abstract expressionism's legacy should be pushed by an agency as powerfully connected as USSALEP. Despite all the claims that African art is primarily geometric, African art has a demonstrably figurative tradition. Its abstract qualities consist in the ideas of continuity and renewal referred to by the various forms of this tradition.

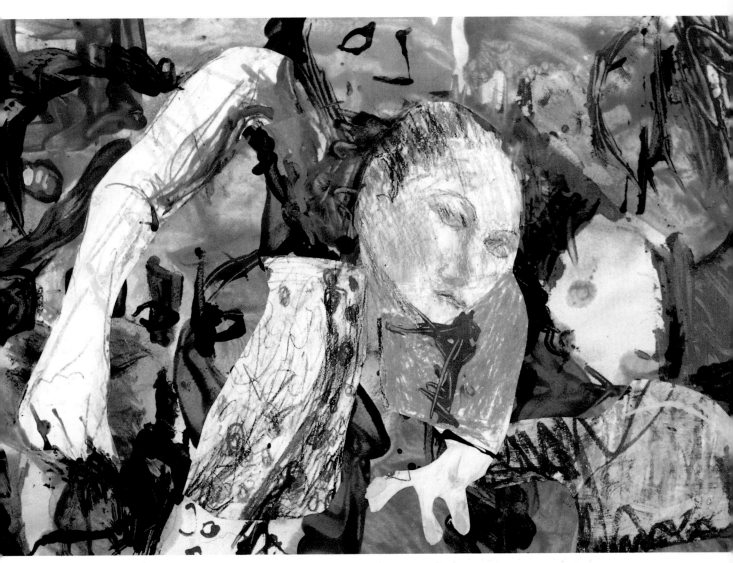

Madam S and her Lover, ink, acrylic and crayon on paper, Mboyi Moshidi, 1987.

Paul Sibisi

Paul Sibisi, who teaches languages at the Umzavela High School, says that he was politicized by his own pupils during the school boycott campaign. 'When I compare their work with mine,' he says, 'they seem so much angrier than I ever was'. The anger he is referring to is not the anger of protest and reportage, which his work epitomizes, but rather the more direct anger of street barricades and boycott. In saying this, he recognizes that their anger is also directed, at least potentially, towards someone like himself. Since other forms of protest against the inferior quality of black education are circumscribed, school children have turned to the devastating tactic of staying away altogether. This hurts themselves, but it also attacks the system as a whole – leaving black teachers in an invidious position.

Sibisi was born in the infamous squatter camp of Cato Manor, or Umkhumbane as it was known to the Zulu-speaking residents who paid rent to Indian landlords. He received a state bursary to study at the Ndaleni Teacher's Training College and in 1972 he was awarded a scholarship by the Institute of Race Relations to study art at the ELC Art Centre. Art is not offered as a subject in many secondary schools and Sibisi took a job teaching language and gave extra lessons in art to interested pupils.

In 1981 his exhibition at the African Art Centre broke new ground; white viewers suddenly saw a reflection of what was going on in the closed world of the townships. His photo-journalistic treatment of police intervention in Umlazi Township also broke new ground technically. It was at this time that he began using a paint atomizer to lay down thin colour washes over his ink drawings. The unusual, perhaps photographically inspired, cropping of his images, gave them added immediacy and when the critic Edward Lucie-Smith

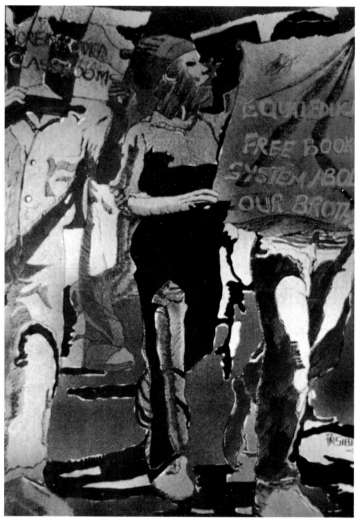

Umzavela Unrest, pen and ink wash on paper, Paul Sibisi, 1981.

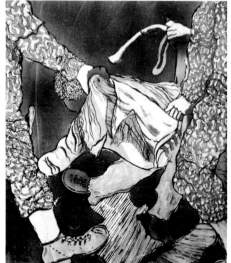

Umzavela Unrest, pen and ink wash on paper, Paul Sibisi, 1981.

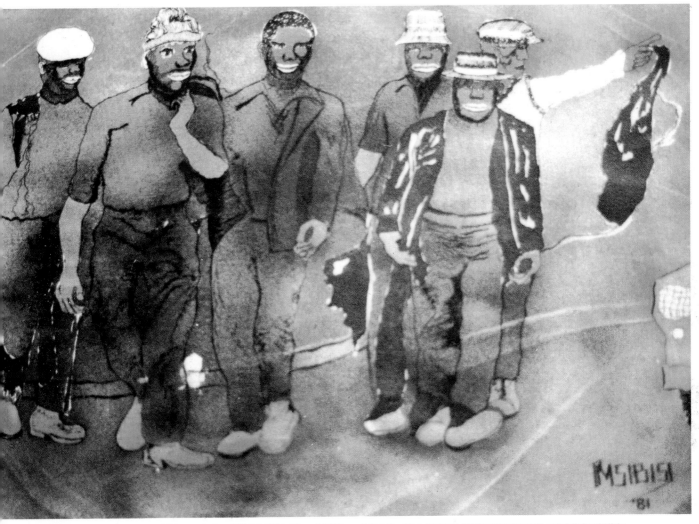

Red Meat Workers' Strike, pen and ink wash, Paul Sibisi, 1981. His exhibition at the Durban African Art Centre in 1981 established Sibis as an artist who was prepared to comment on political events. In the largely apolitical milieu of the art world, his reportage of industrial action and 'unrest' appeared refreshingly direct. Drawing on his own and photographic sources, Sibisi's gentle form of social realism has earned him a prestigious British Council fellowship.

asked to be shown the work of some black artists, it was Paul Sibisi he was taken to see. Lucie-Smith had come out to judge the 1981 Republic Art Festival only to find that many South African artists, including Sibisi, were boycotting the celebrations.

Sibisi describes the background to the series entitled *Umzavela Unrest* in this way: 'During the class boycotts at my school, the pupils marched on the streets and it continued until camouflaged policemen came to stop the demonstrations. Then the "outside element" joined the pupils and they used the demonstrations as an opportunity to loot shops and stores. The police got tough on everyone, even if they found small groups of students meeting – they broke them up and stated that no meetings could be held without permission. All students would then be punished if they assembled in groups, whether they meant harm or not. I am trying to show someone being punished, someone not intending to do harm.'

His painting entitled *Red Meat Workers' Strike* (the red boots are standard abattoir issue) is characteristically anecdotal. Paul Sibisi acknowledges the influence of the nineteenth-century satirists (among them, Honoré Daumier, whose work he saw in reproduction whilst studying at Ndaleni College) but claims that his imagery is not politically motivated. 'Artists should be above politics. I'm depicting what is happening on the street, the way I see it.'

David Hlongwane

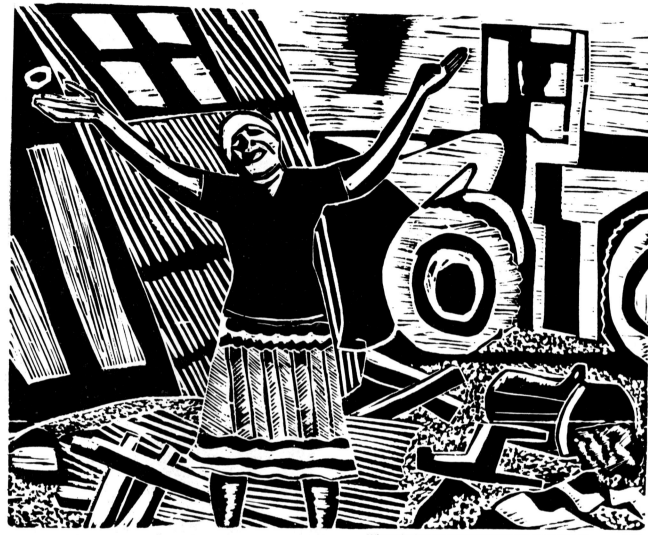

Where to Go?, linoleum relief print, David Hlongwane, 1986.

Issues of legitimation cut across the spectrum of cultural activity and in 1981 the Republic Art Festival committee achieved a coup in persuading a prominent English critic to judge a competition celebrating twenty years of the South African Republic. Many South African artists boycotted this art festival because of its official governmental links, yet Edward Lucie-Smith, the critic, only commented approvingly on the work of black artists who boycotted the competition. Perhaps this action helped him to legitimate his own position in the growing storm over the cultural boycott. Other foreign embassies enter the legitimation stakes with their own education programmes weighted in favour of blacks. In the scramble for legitimacy, black support for whatever programme is being offered is seen as an indication of its success or failure. This focus often draws attention away from the 'specifics of patronage' and leaves neo-colonial interventions more or less intact.

However, the legitimation problems of these programmes are insignificant when compared to the white suprematist convictions of the South African Government. A national art conference held in Stellenbosch in April 1988, aimed at addressing 'special problems', had an organizing committee, under the chairmanship of Dr Jan Schutte, which did not include one black person.

The different regions, however, do have different approaches to the issues of legitimation and accountability. For instance, the Western Cape has the reputation of being more 'political'. David Hlongwane, a relatively unknown black artist, was chosen as the region's delegate to the Culture in Another South Africa (CASA) conference held in Amsterdam in December 1987. Most of the other regions, in contrast, chose established artists.

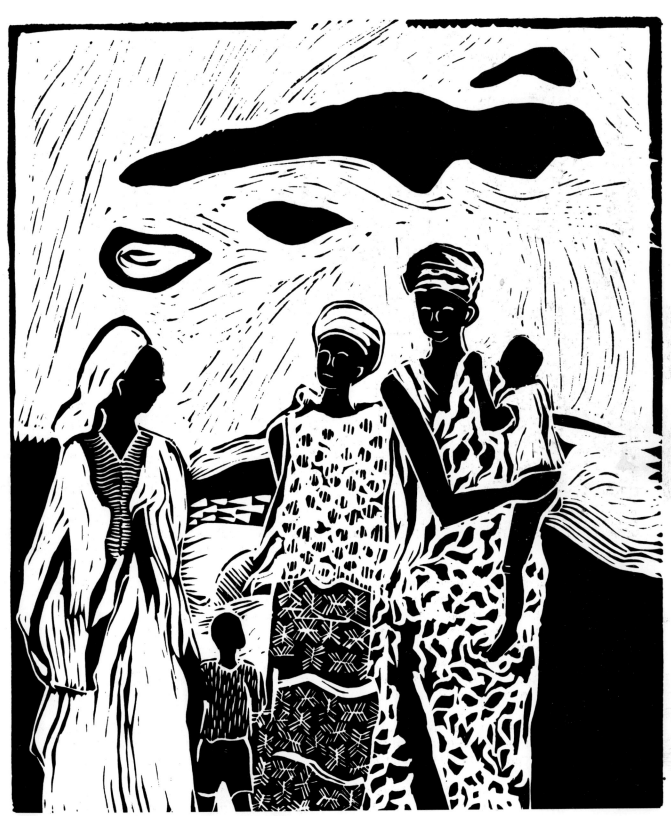

Get Together, linoleum relief print, Hamilton Budaza, 1983.

Sfiso Mkame

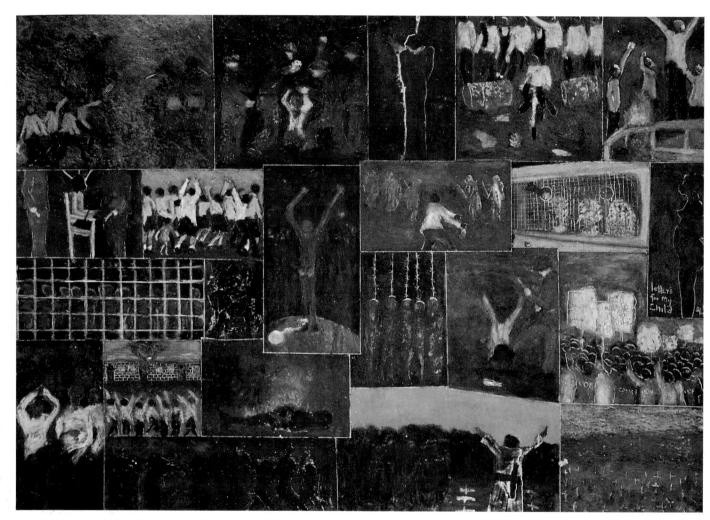

Letters to my Child, oil pastel on paper, Sfiso Mkame, 1987.

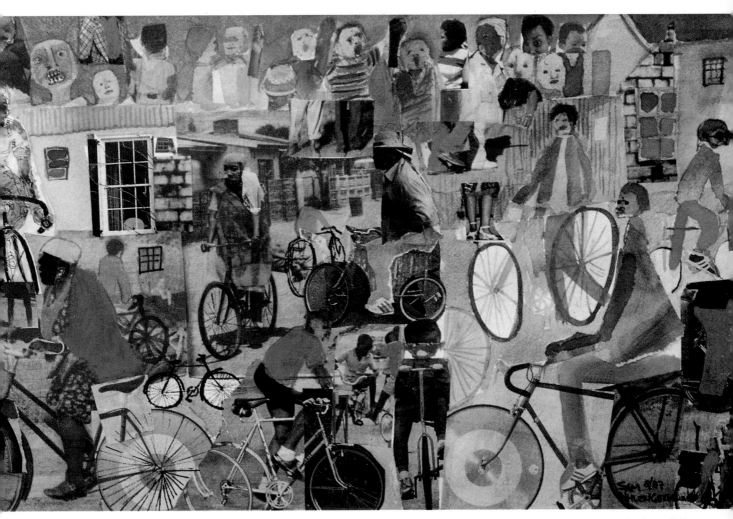

Putco Strike, acrylic, collage on paper, Sam Nhlengethwa, 1987.

Peter Clarke

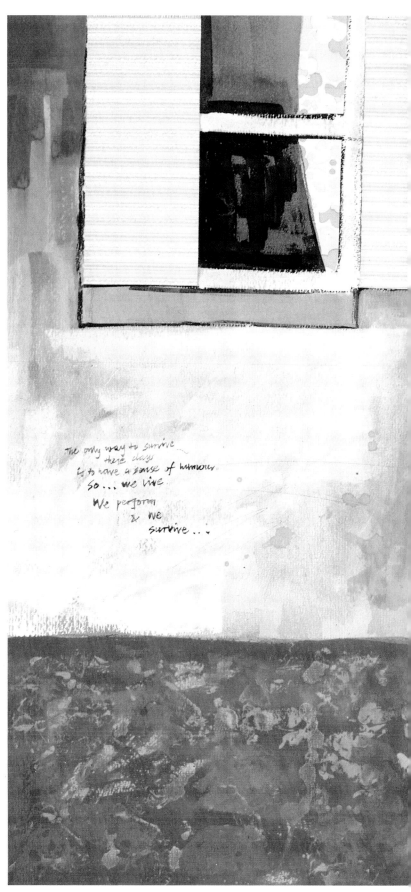

The Only Way to Survive, acrylic and ink on board, Peter Clarke, 1983.

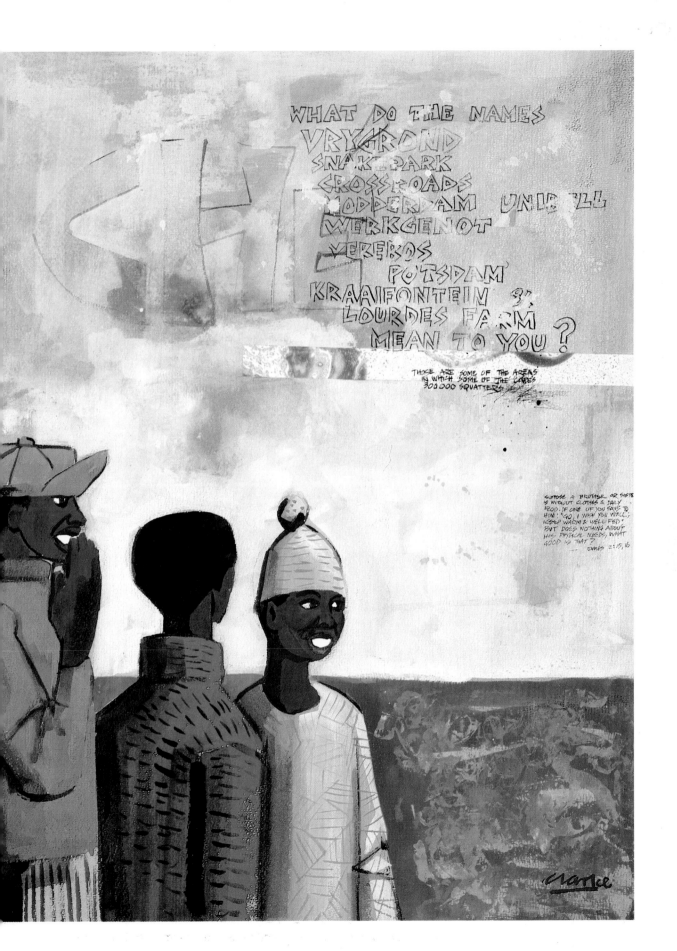

Avashoni Mainganye

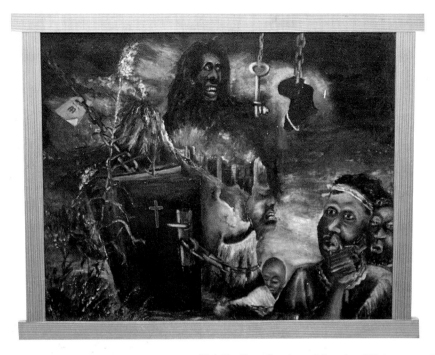

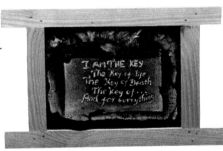

I Am the Key, oil on board, Avashoni Mainganye, 1985.

Heart in the Oven, woodblock relief print, Avashoni Mainganye, 1982.

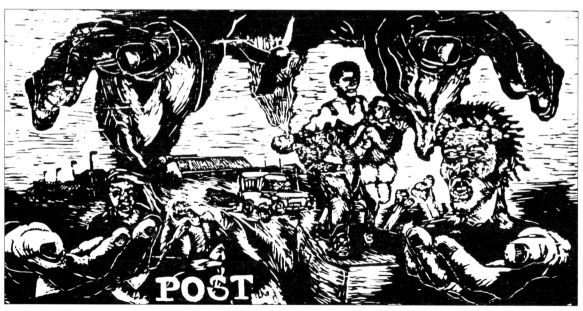

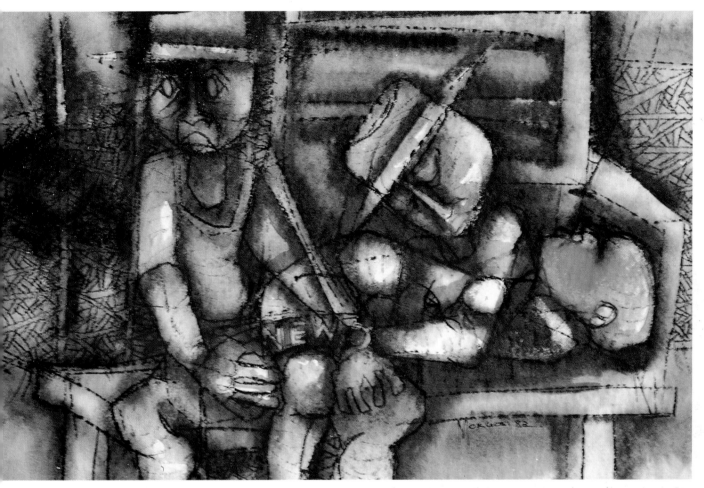

Unemployed, ink and charcoal on paper, Nat Mokgotsi, 1985.

Sydney Holo

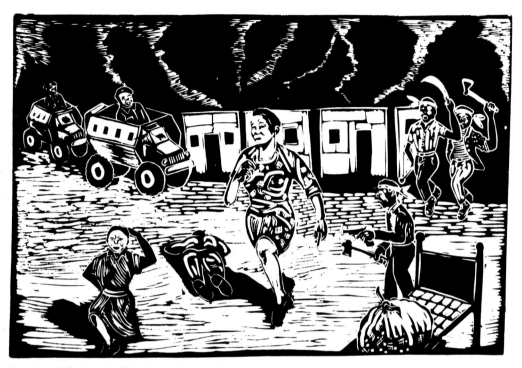

Crossroads, linoleum relief print, Sydney Holo, 1986.

Holo's image of the reign of vigilante terrorism which has struck squatter communities repeatedly in recent years is heightened by the awkward clarity of the drawing. Holo witnessed the struggle between the vigilante 'witdoeke' ('white scarves') and the 'comrades' from the Nyanga Arts Centre where he teaches. Affidavits filed by church leaders who witnessed the 'burn out' of part of Crossroads claim that the security forces stood by, and in certain cases actually assisted the vigilantes. This allegation is confirmed in Holo's rendering of the impassive presence of the army in their toy-like 'Buffels'.

Thamsanqwa Mnyele

Although Mnyele's drawings are guided by a realistic intention, he frequently leaves part of his figures undrawn. In this way he interpolates his own extreme introspection. A metaphysical reading of his drawings is also encouraged by their scrubbed and bruised surface. According to his associates, he often rubbed dirt into the paper to deepen the illusion of space and to make a gesture of protest against the commercialism he left behind him when he abandoned his career in advertising to go into exile.

Thamsanqwa Mnyele wanted to be an artist from the age of fourteen and his parents sent him to the ELC Art and Craft Centre in Rorke's Drift. Here he gained a working knowledge of printmaking techniques and after he left South Africa in 1979 he helped form the Medu Art Ensemble which specialized in protest posters. He was shot dead in his sleep during a cross-border raid by the South African Defence Force on suspected ANC houses in Botswana on 14 June 1985.

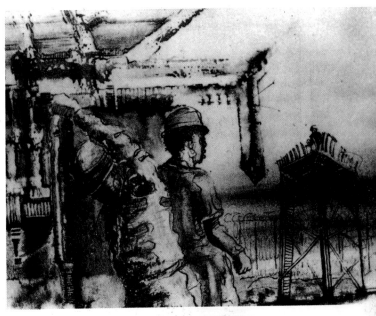

Untitled, pencil on paper, Thamsanqwa Mnyele, 1980.

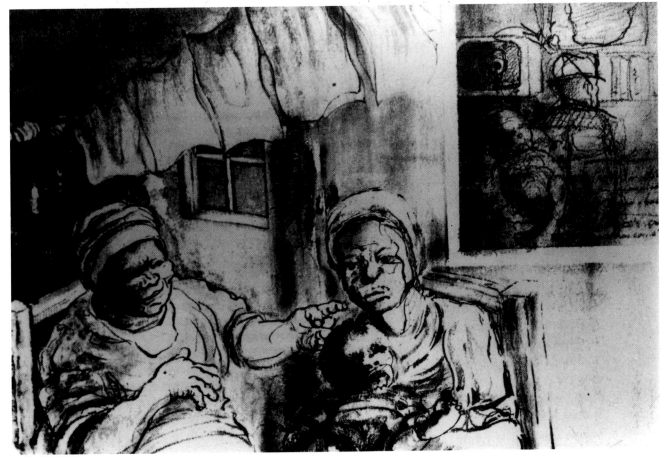

Untitled, pencil on paper, Thamsanqwa Mnyele, 1980.

Jackson Hlungwani

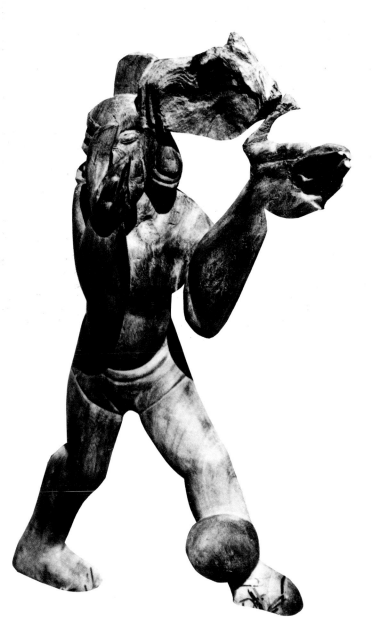

Seeing Straight, kiaat wood, Jackson Hlungwani, 1985.

Jackson Hlungwani's residence can only be reached on foot. A pile of abandoned carvings leaning against a wild fig tree announces the start of a path which leads up to the ruins of the Karmi structure in which he has been living, and to which he has been adding since he moved to the area from Mashampa nearly two decades ago. No mortar has been used in the meticulous stonemasonry; even the windows have been built without the help of mud or clay to support the large stone lintels. Although a rough thatch covers the building, Hlungwani holds religious services outdoors in a large stone circle fronted by an altar. Not all of the other enclosures are used, but one of them has become what he calls an 'office' and in 1984 it contained a single sculpture.

Closer inspection of this sculpture reveals an impenetrable image of a whale-like fish swimming easily with the current and supported on a carved axle. Ventral, pectoral and dorsal fins are all sharply defined and have parallel grooves which follow the twisting movement of the body. Since there are no large rivers in the vicinity, the viewer is left puzzled as to the sculpture's meaning.

Jackson Hlungwani has said that his work does not originate in himself but that 'it comes from God Himself, and from the Lord, and from the Holy Spirit.' He is not only referring to his sculpture, but also to his evangelical work as the overseer of an African Independent Church called 'Yesu Geleliya One Apostle in Sayoni Alt and Omega'. Works like his *Fish* make an impact in any environment, but Hlungwani's placement of this piece, in a chapel-like structure, alerts the viewer to its symbolic overtones. However, the fish form itself has deep religious significance. The motif of the fish has been used as a plastic symbol in the art of Africa since at least 3500 B.C. A clay fish lying on a square plate, now in the Ashmolean Museum in Oxford, was made in Egypt at about this time. Pagan cults of the fish in western Asia probably had their origin in ceremonies designed to assure a bountiful catch and the image of priest as fisher predates its Christian counterparts. Christ is both Divine Fish and 'fisher of men'. Reborn through immersion, the convert swallows the Eucharist, thus affirming salvation. For Jung, the motif of the fish operates not as a sign, but rather in the true sense of a symbol, that is, as a way of describing something that is not completely knowable.

A statement by Hlungwani draws attention to the religious significance of his fish imagery. Asked about the meaning of this carving, Hlungwani replied: 'Oh My name, I'm fish.' Asked if he had ever seen such a fish he replied that he had not, but that his heart 'caught' all things. Theo Schneider and Sikheto Daniel Maluleke of the Tsonga Bible Translation Project recorded one of his Tsonga services which showed that Hlungwani fully believes that God works through him:

'Well this work of mine, what I am doing now, is not an image; it is not an idea, it is not a fairy-tale. It is truth itself . . . The reason is that this work of mine does not originate in me.'

Although Hlungwani frequently refers to Christ as the source of life he makes little use of central Gospel themes. Instead, as Schneider notes, he dwells on one recurrent apocalyptic vision. 'Heaven and Hell are about to be radically transfigured, and mankind will open its eyes. The old world of sin and strife is about to be replaced by the new world of forgiveness and brotherhood.'

Hlungwani's woodcut is a graphic depiction of this vision and shows what he calls a 'map for first country, map for new country.' Within the rows of domestic animals, the artist has grouped all the symbols of the cosmic order around a tree of life 'whose leaves are for the healing of the nations'. The theme of an apocalyptic social transformation is taken up in narrative and descriptive form in all his major works with the possible exception of *Fish* where he relies on an embedded symbolism. His carving entitled *Gabriel* makes use of the stylistic device of reversed depth – instead of the eyes being recessed, they are shown as protruberances. Narrow horizontal cuts detail the pupils. There is no suggestion in the form that he has worked from illustrations in religious handbooks; the figure of the angel Gabriel is unmistakably African. When he was asked about the sword his tone of voice became crestfallen: 'This is sword for fighting, but we don't want fighting no more.'

In the larger, magisterial carving of *Cain* the artist has produced his finest work. Here there is no hesitation in the way in which he has controlled volume; even the original form of the wood has not dictated its terms. Once again there is a depiction of a sword: 'This is hand of God. Tell us – No more fighting. If you try to fight, myself I hit it.' Another statement by Hlungwani leads one to believe that his emphasis on the apocalyptic aspects of Christianity stems from a desire to come to terms with his negative experiences as a migrant worker in Johannesburg. The son of a mine worker, Hlungwani lost his finger and his job in an industrial accident. He was upset at not receiving compensation after being maimed while performing a skilled job at unskilled wages; he did not, however, seem to mind losing his job, reasoning that any machine that started with a finger could easily end up demanding an arm, 'So I must come home, work for myself and make my soul better'. This was in 1944. In 1946 he was ordained as a priest in the African Zionist Church; he had found a way of sublimating poverty and oppression.

Sublimation is also evident in the small carving, *Seeing Straight*. Since 1978, Hlungwani has been plagued by an open sore on his right leg which will not heal. Although he has been treated at the nearby Elim Hospital, this lesion has not responded to treatment.

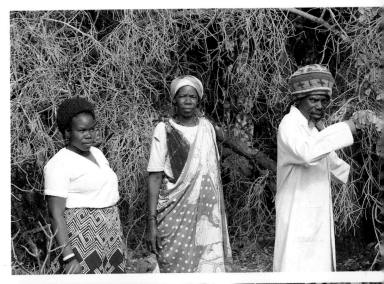

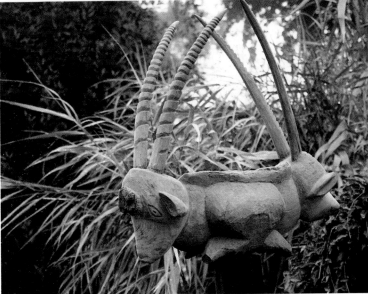

Above top: Jackson, Magdalena and Palatsini Hlungwani at Mashampa, 1987.

Above: untitled, wood, Jackson Hlungwani, 1985.

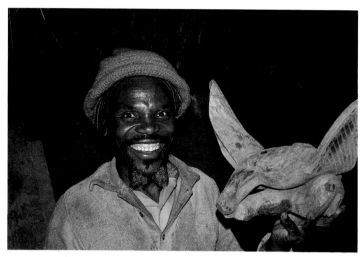

Jackson Hlungwani, photographed 1984.

Hlungwani also spent many years working in an asbestos mine near Pietersburg. Unlike some of his fellow workers, he has not yet contracted mesothelomia, but the possibility of malignancy in his lesions exists. This affliction has entered his consciousness to such a degree that ball-shaped lumps appear on the lower leg of this sculpture, as well as on a number of others. The idea that events in the real world can be affected by making effigies is by no means a new one in African art. In Jackson Hlungwani's case, he has adopted the Christian idea of substitution (Christ dying so that man/woman may be reborn) with such absolute conviction that he sees no distinction between his *Crucifixion* and real events in history.

In a way, *Seeing Straight* is an idealized self-portrait. We see a man pointing forward with his whole body. Hands with long, outstretched fingers guide the man's gaze forward, like the blinders on a carthorse. But the real exhortation, to 'see straight', derives from a curious protruberance of raw, unworked wood which rises from the subject's head. This, according to Hlungwani, is the 'map' by means of which people must live their lives. It is not a concrete representation of abstract thought, but life prefigured.

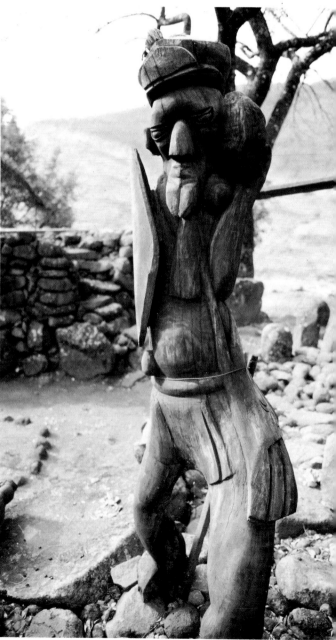

Cain, carved konono wood, Jackson Hlungwani, *c.*1980.

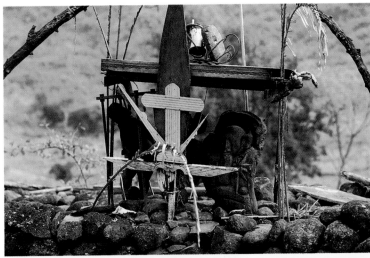

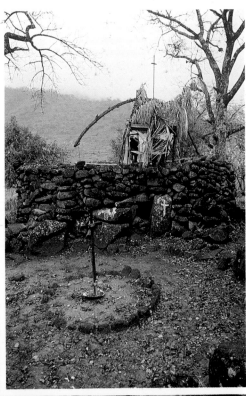

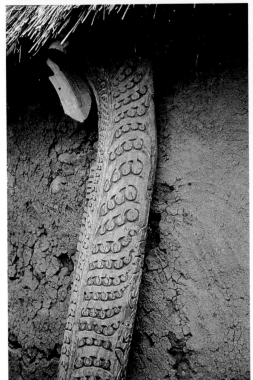

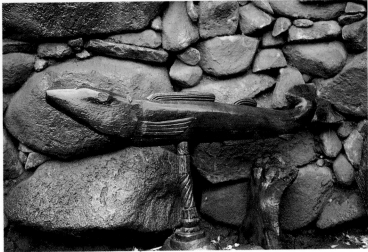

Left above: Yesu Geleliya One Apostle in Sayoni Alt and Omega, altar, 1986.

Above top: Yesu Geleliya One Apostle in Sayoni Alt and Omega, chapel, 1986.

Left: carved panel, wood, Jackson Hlungwani, *c.*1984.

Above: *Fish*, carved konono wood, Jackson Hlungwani, *c.*1983.

Jim Ngumo

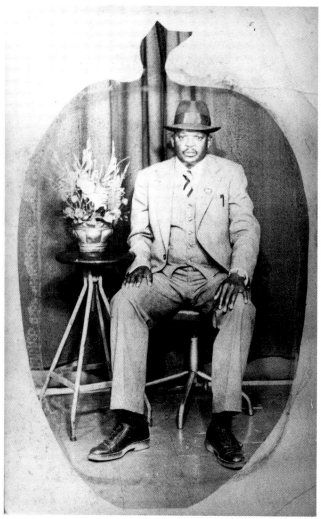

Jim Ngumo.

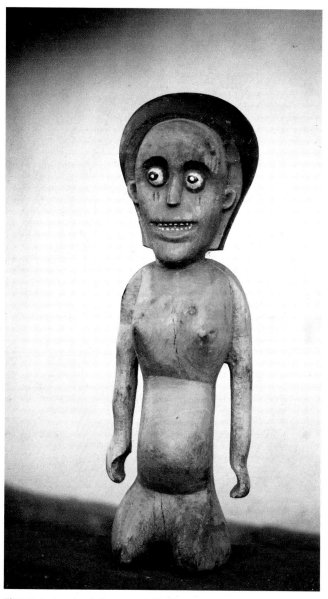

Figure, enamel paint on wood, Jim Ngumo, *c.*1985.

African art is embedded in its social context to such a degree that the specific focus of art criticism or review always appears dangerously superficial. A purely art historical approach does not have the conceptual categories to analyse a series of woodcarvings which resulted in their maker being killed. What criteria are we going to use to discuss the carving illustrated above when it is learnt that it is one of a number of sculptures which led to Jim Ngumo being fatally attacked by a group of people from his village on 18 May 1986?

From reports, it has become clear that the villagers were convinced that his carvings of small animals and tall cylindrical figures were in some way responsible for their misfortune and that the artist was exerting spells through this medium. Leaving aside the temptation to speculate on the anthropological significance of the works, the

carvings undoubtedly deserve recognition as art. The most striking aspect of the artist's reductive analysis of the volumes of the body is to be found in the low relief of the woman's face against the planes of her neck. Despite the loss of the arms in a fire started by the artist's attackers, the engorged shoulder pads and the fact that the eyelids have been peeled away leaving the orbs of the eyes exposed hint at the piece's once compelling intensity.

The Ngumo family refused permission for photographs to be taken of his small, outwardly unremarkable, carvings of frogs and it is these which are considered to be specially potent in exorcizing strong spirits which are in possession of the body.

Opposite: figure, enamel paint on wood, Jim Ngumo, *c.*1985.

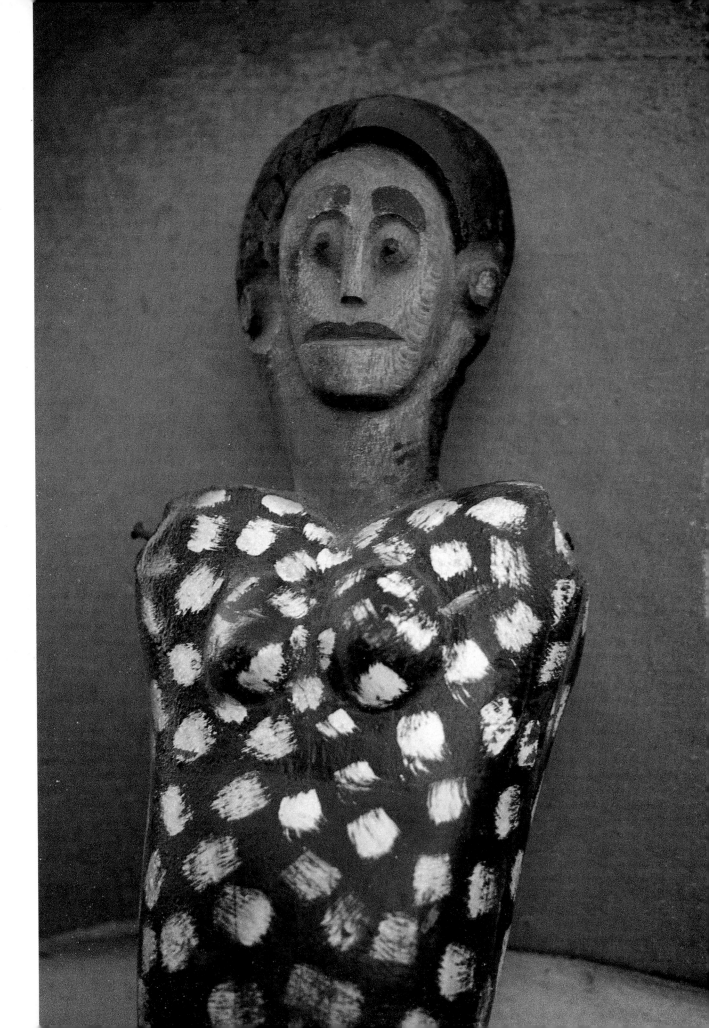

John Muafangejo

'My illness? One day the Minister invited me to eat by him. One man working there was jealous, he put poison in the beer. That gave me a heart condition that makes my head work more.'

John Muafangejo died as a result of complications arising from high blood pressure on 27 November 1987. He was working at his house at 5481 Gamand in Katutura and was due to travel to Cape Town the following week to discuss plans for a commission at the University of the Western Cape. He had also spent the last six months preparing for a major retrospective of his work at the Standard Bank Festival of the Arts in Grahamstown in 1988. At 44, Muafangejo is the youngest artist to have been awarded this distinction and it is difficult to think of an artist whose work is so universally admired. The harshest comments directed towards his work relate to the sometimes messy printing and the cheap, sixty-gram bond paper that he used for his linoleum relief prints.

Muafangejo's work is strongly autobiographical and he often includes written observations on the events he portrays in his prints. What began as a labelling device after his return from his second stay at Rorke's Drift in 1975 quickly took on an important supplementary function. Whilst the text in *Battle of Rorke's Drift* (1981) is little more than a title, his *New Archbishop Desmond Tutu Enthroned* (1986) (see p. 7) includes a prayer asking for God's help. This meshing of two narrative structures, text and image, gives his work a topical currency and, on occasion, historical importance. Although the artist often represents historical events through the medium of conventional historical records, for instance his *Battle of Rorke's Drift*, he also sometimes records events with the insights of someone who was involved. The artist has said that his style is 'a teaching style' and that he always uses black 'because it doesn't tire the eyes'. Prints like *Battle of Rorke's Drift* are easy to look at and they are interesting in their formal discontinuities. For Muafangejo, the dead are simply horizontal warriors, as bright-eyed as any of the others.

This emotional aloofness is honest. The artist is not trying to shake every last cent of guilt from his white audience. There is, however, another trade-off for which the artist cannot be held responsible. His comments are usually made in broken English and the quaintness of his expression hijacks the political impact of his work and consigns it to the timeless and ahistorical realm of folk art. Thus, in *New Archbishop Desmond Tutu Enthroned* we are told that

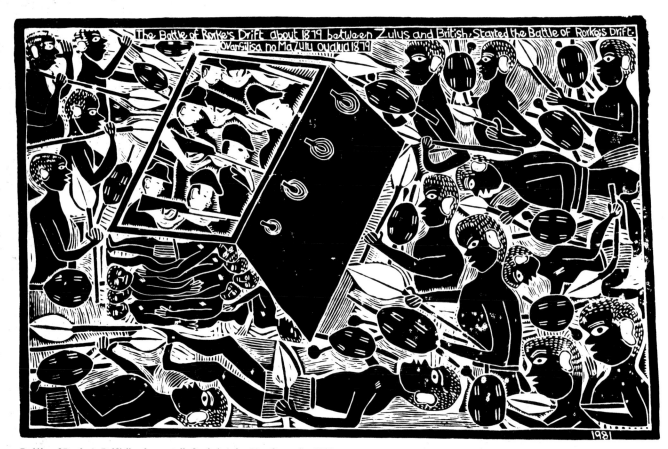

Battle of Rorke's Drift, linoleum relief print, John Muafangejo, 1981.

Opposite: *St. Antonius Hospital*, linoleum relief print, John Muafangejo, 1987.

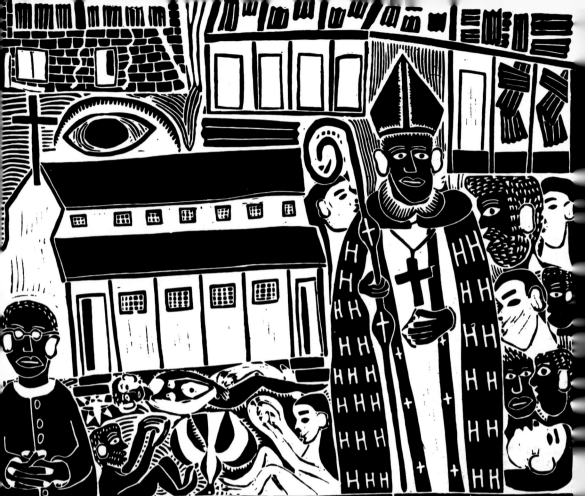

ANGLICAN SEMINARY BLOWN UP: The Seminary blown up by Bombing by Master no body. This building was destroyed by un Known People on Thursday 18-6-1981 at 1.a.m. It is near the border of Namibia and Angola. This destruction is the 3rd of St. Mary's building those were same about like that one.

(1) House of archdeacon in 1975 (2) House of Priest, Engineering for lite house and carpentery work shop in 1979. The Eighth Bishop Rt. J.H. Kauluma was Preaching in Saddness together with his Archdeacon Revd. P.H. Shilongo for the destroyed houses of Odibo MISSION. Bishop will be Rebuild them one day but we are Anglican, Christians, let us thing, when wo will got same helpful to our Bishop beause it is not new tring. It is Old action which was going slow by slowly. If we are truly Christian faithy. We must give 10% of our Properties to Bishop when he will ready for Rebuild the three deferents builds Please, As what ANGLICAN NAMIBIA ARTIST FULFIL LIKE AMEN. JOHN 7:37-45.

(OMuBISOFI Wotu OKu-audifa noluhodi unene Molomile ei. Vakuetu Ovaholike tupasukeni Ose Si Pamba oKue Lilongi Kida Omolomanjonauno etu. Ohele ei jaua Palola Kalunga. Esi osili osikolo savamue velihonga no vapita Most mary's Odibo Ei sho longhenda la Pamba. Kalunga Otatale no neni kuvo omutenja no ufiku. Epulo lange Kunje oleli ile Elombuelo Kunje jandjeni sa Omaongalo a ese andja modibo. Ku Bishofi wongeleka jai Ngilikana okukuafela oku tu-ngulula omatungilo a dibo o sesi ojo indje ngeleka adise Mowambo sandja Komufaneki wongeleka.)

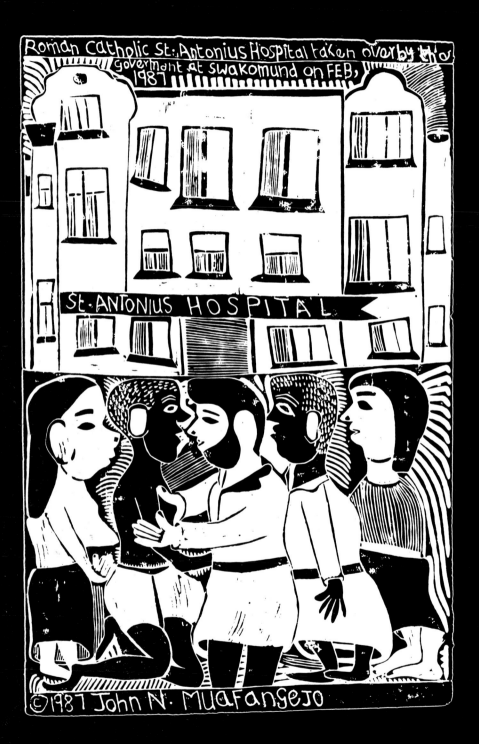

The congregation 'was praying and plodding' and in *Oniipa New Printing Press and Book Depot* we learn that the old press was burnt down by 'master nobody'. In the wake of so much hard news reporting on Namibia, his broken English is not without its appeal.

John Ndevasia Muafangejo was born in the Kwanjama village of Etunda lo Nghadi, Southern Angola, in 1943. The international boundary between Namibia and Angola passes through Kwanjama territory and after the death of his father in 1956, Muafangejo left Angola on foot to join other members of his family at St Mary's Mission at Odibo in Namibia. His talent and his deep religious conviction was noticed by Bishop Mallory who arranged for a bursary for Muafangejo to study at the Evangelical Lutheran Church (ELC) Art and Craft Centre at Rorke's Drift. He went there in 1967 and completed the course two years later. In 1971, in the first of a series of local and international distinctions, one of his prints was chosen for display at the Sâo Paulo Biennial. During this period Muafangejo had returned to St Mary's Mission where he gave art lessons until 1974 when he returned to the ELC Art and Craft Centre for a refresher course.

By the early 1980s Muafangejo was exhibiting regularly abroad. In 1980 his work was shown in Finland; in 1982 his work was accepted for the International Print Biennial in Reading and in 1983 at the Commonwealth Institute, London. This exhibition prompted comparisons between his work and that of leading German Expressionists and that of David Hockney. He was also honoured in South Africa and his work *Angolaland – South West Africa 1976* won a prize in the Republic Art Festival in 1981. This festival was widely boycotted by artists and Muafangejo's presence there is typical of the man who has said, 'I am not a political person. It is the world which is political'.

This is not to say that the artist avoids political events. A number of prints deal with the bombing of church buildings at Oniipa. The image of Bishop Kauluma outside the boarded-up windows of the seminary at Odibo in *Anglican Seminary Blown Up* is a catechism on the principle of Christian forgiveness. In many other prints, notably *New Archbishop Desmond Tutu Enthroned* and *Activity Centre*, black and white people are shown shaking hands in 'love and co-operation'. This was Muafangejo's message to the world. It was a simple message that deserved to be heeded in 1980 when he painstakingly cut the letters in reverse out of the linoleum. It was not heeded then and shows no sign of having made any impression since that time.

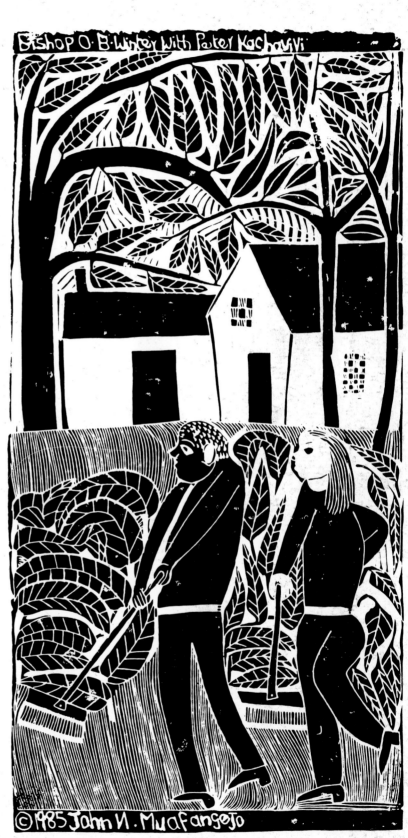

Bishop O.B. Winter with Peter Kachavivi, linoleum relief print, John Muafangejo, 1985.

Biographies

Khulekile Hamilton BUDAZA page 75
Born on 8 March 1958 in Kensington, Cape Town. His father worked in Cape Town on contract and he attended primary school in Ciskei. He completed his Junior Certificate in 1976 at Langa High School. He joined the Community Arts Project soon after it was established in 1977. He has exhibited regularly in group exhibitions in the Western Cape and is presently a teacher in CAP's out-reach programme at the Luyolo Centre in Guguletu.

Peter CLARKE page 78
Born in 1929 in Simonstown. Completed a BA(Fine Art) at the Michaelis School of Art, University of Cape Town, in 1961. Spent the next two years at the Rijks Academie van Beeldende Kunsten in Amsterdam. Has illustrated many books and won the Drum International Short Story Award in 1955. Awarded a fellowship in writing from the University of Iowa and an honorary doctorate from the World Academy of Arts and Culture in Taipei. He now lives in Ocean View and is a professional artist and writer.

Lionel DAVIS page 10
Born in 1936 in Cape Town. Completed the ninth year of schooling at Harold Cressy High School in Zonnebloem. In 1964 he was convicted and imprisoned for five years on Robben Island under the Suppression of Communism Act. In prison he developed an interest in writing. He experienced difficulty in getting employment and worked sporadically as a clerk and storeman. In 1978 he discovered the Community Arts Project by chance and immediately enrolled. In 1980 CAP organized a bursary for him to study at the ELC Art and Craft Centre at Rorke's Drift. He is now a full-time organizer at CAP.

Bongiwe DHLOMO page 24
Born on 25 June 1956 at the Lutheran Mission, Vryheid. Her father was a Lutheran minister and the family moved frequently. By 1974 she had completed her high school education. In 1975 she completed a year's secretarial training at the Inanda Seminary and worked for two years before going to the ELC Art and Craft Centre where she qualified at the end of 1979. Thereafter she worked at the Durban Art Centre and the Federated Union of Black Arts. She is now the director of the Alexandra Arts Centre.

Smart GUMEDE page 20
Born on 19 November 1943 in Ndwedwe, Natal. He completed his primary and secondary school education in Ndwedwe before training as a teacher at the Amanzintoti Teacher Training College. His talent was discovered by Ms Nguza and in 1977 he received a specialist Art Teacher's Certificate from Ndeleni Teacher Training College. Meanwhile he obtained his matriculation certificate through Damelin Correspondence College. In 1983 he began studying for a BA(Fine Art) through Fort Hare University and after a break in 1986, he qualified at the end of 1987.

Zamokwakhe GUMEDE page 49
Born on 8 August 1955 at Emnjaneni, Natal. He completed his lower-primary school education and worked in various jobs until 1980 when he started carpentry classes at Mariannhill Monastery. His first carvings were bought on consignment by the African Art Centre.

Randy HARTZENBERG page 67
Born on 8 March 1948 in Cape Town. He matriculated from Alexander Sinton Senior Secondary School in 1965 and completed a Senior School Art Teacher's Diploma at the Hewatt Teachers' Training College in 1968. During this time he was taught by Amos Langdown. Hartzenberg then taught art at Alexander Sinton until 1985, when he enrolled for a degree in Fine Art at the University of Cape Town. He was involved with the innovative programmes of the Space Gallery during the late 1970s and put on a number of installations.

Sambona Sipho Nt'sali HLATI page 19
Born on 14 January 1963 in Guguletu, Cape Town. He attended school at Fezeka High School in Guguletu and completed his secondary schooling at St Francis High School, Langa, in 1985. He helped organize Community Arts Project classes in the townships before enrolling for the three-year full-time course at CAP in 1987. He has exhibited in a number of politically oriented art exhibitions but prefers to exhibit at township venues. He is actively involved in attempts to establish township-based art facilities.

David Tsolwane Uhuru HLONGWANE page 74
Born on 1 January 1963 at Zwelethemba Township, Worcester. He completed his high school education at Vuyisile High School in Worcester and joined the Community Arts Project in 1984 which he read about in *Grassroots*, a community newspaper. In 1985 his brother, who was supporting him, was allegedly killed by the police during a demonstration and he had to give up his studies.

Jackson HLUNGWANI page 84
Born in 1923 at Mashampa Village, Transvaal. His father was recruited into the mines. He never went to school and learnt to speak English and Afrikaans while working, first as a labourer, and then as a packer for various companies. He lost his finger in an industrial accident while working for the Springfield Coffee Company. In 1946 he started an African independent church and preaches from his stone-walled 'New Jerusalem' at Mbhokota.

Sydney HOLO pages 25, 82
Born in 1952 in Belville, Cape Town. Completed his Higher-Primary School Certificate at Vakhanya Primary School in Guguletu. In 1979 he helped establish the Nyanga Art Centre. He now teaches ceramics, painting and graphics at the centre.

David KOLOANE page 23
Born on 5 June 1938 in Alexandra Township, Johannesburg. His father's illness prevented him from completing the second year of his high school education at Orlando High School. At school he met Louis Maqhubela who continued to encourage him during the fifteen years he spent working in various clerical positions. Maqhubela introduced him to Bill Ainslie and he studied with Ainslie from 1974 until 1977 when he founded the first Black Art Gallery with Bidi and Nolutshungu. In 1982 he was appointed Head of Fine Art at FUBA and won a bursary to study at the Birmingham Polytechnic in 1983. He spent the next two years in England at the University of London completing a Diploma in Museum Studies. He is now Curator of the FUBA Gallery.

Sydney KUMALO page 22
Born in 1935 in Johannesburg. He studied art under Cecil Skotnes at the Polly Street Art Centre and taught there when the centre moved to the Jubilee Centre. He has received numerous sculpture commissions and has won a number of prizes since he first won the Philip Frame award on the first Art SA Today Exhibition in 1963.

Suzanne LOUW pages 16, 17
Born on 29 November 1964 in Cape Town. She completed her primary schooling at Wynberg Primary School and her secondary education at Herschel High School in Cape Town. Qualified in 1986 for a BA(Fine Art) at Michaelis School of Art, University of Cape Town.

Luthando LUPUWANA page 69
Born on 24 December 1954 at Nqamakwe, Transkei. He lived with his parents in the Bo-Kaap in Cape Town until 1962 when African families were moved out of mixed-race areas into the townships. This severely disadvantaged his father who was a tailor. Believing that the township schools were too disruptive his parents sent him to schools in Transkei. After working as a clerk and labourer for seven years he enrolled at the University of Fort Hare in 1979 for a degree in Fine Art. In 1981 he transferred to the University of Cape Town where he completed his degree and a post-graduate diploma in printmaking. During 1986 and 1987 he ran informal art classes in the townships as part of the Community Arts Project's out-reach programme.

Noria MABASA page 38
Born on 10 May 1938 at Tshigalo Village, Venda. She did not attend school and found a job as a domestic worker with a farmer near Louis Trichardt. In the late 1970s she became a full-time artist and lives and works at Tshino Village. Her clay is dug from the local river bank and her work is fired in the traditional manner in a straw fire. Her husband, a migrant worker, was murdered in Alexandra Township in May 1987.

Marta MAHLANGU page 56
Born on 11 October 1934 on Jakkalsfontein Farm near Bronkhorstspruit, Marta Mahlangu received a traditional schooling and later became a member of the African Zionist Church at Mabhokho. Weltvreden, the area in which she now lives was born is part of the farm which was bought in 1923 by Chief Nyabela's followers as an ancestral home after the dispersal of the Southern Ndebele people following the disastrous 1883 war against the Boer government. In 1972 this farm formed the nucleus of the KwaNdebele 'homeland' and is now the seat of Chief David Mahlangu. The artist is not related to the Chief.

Sarah MAHLANGU page 30
Born about 1958 at Mabhokho, KwaNdebele. She received a traditional schooling and, like all young women, Sarah Mahlangu learned the art of wall painting from her mother. However, she gained more experience than most women because her mother, Francina Ndimande, received a commission to decorate the local Roman Catholic out-station. Sarah Mahlangu and her sister were asked to help.

Avashoni MAINGANYE page 80
Born on 11 November 1957 at Tshivhasa Village, Venda. After matriculating from Khwevha High School he gained entrance to the ELC Art and Craft Centre in 1981. In 1985 he entered the full-time art programme at FUNDA Centre and is studying towards a BA(Fine Art) through the University of South Africa.

Mathew 'MK' MALEFANE page 15
Born on 29 March 1958 in Soweto. Malefane attended a number of church schools in Lesotho before matriculating from Lesotho High School in 1975. He is a self-taught artist and in 1985 studied film-making techniques under John Hill in Cape Town. He has been active in plans to start a second film school in South Africa and is now a documentary film-maker in Johannesburg.

Boyisile (Billy) MANDINDI pages 17, 62
Born on 24 February 1967 in Guguletu Township, Cape Town. He finished the first year of high school at Ntaba-Kandoda High School in Ciskei. He spent 1985 and 1986 in the full-time art programme at the Community Arts Project under Lucy Alexander. In 1987 he enrolled for a degree in Fine Arts at the Michaelis School of Art, University of Cape Town.

Craig Stewart MASTERS page 68
Born on 29 July 1962 in Cape Town. He matriculated from Alexander Sinton Senior Secondary School in 1983 and thereafter studied art under Emile Maurice at the Battswood Art Centre on a part-time basis for the next two years. He is interested in capturing the contrasts in South African life and has shown his work in a number of politically oriented exhibitions in the Western Cape.

Johannes MASWANGANYI page 42
Born in July 1949 in Msengi Village, Gazankulu. He went to school at the nearby Haaka School in Noblehoek. He learned to carve from his father who was a professional woodcarver. His first carvings were functional objects and he sold his first spoon in 1965. There was a strong local demand for wooden bowls, spoons and *nyamisoro* but after the BMW Tributaries exhibition in Johannesburg in 1985 his market changed. He now lives and works as a full-time artist at Noblehoek.

Emile MAURICE page 66
Born on 30 June 1955 in Cape Town. Matriculated at Harold Cressy High School in Zonnebloem in 1972. Obtained a BA(Fine Art) and an Advanced Diploma from the Michaelis School of Art, University of Cape Town, in 1979 and taught at the Hewatt Teachers' Training College. In 1981 he obtained an MA from Syracuse University. On his return to South Africa he taught at the Battswood Art Centre until 1987. He is now an Education Officer at the South African National Gallery.

Leya MGUNI page 57
Born about 1934 on a farm near Rayton in the district of Pretoria. Leya Mguni's family works for white farmers and she learned to speak and write Afrikaans on local farm schools. Eight years ago her daughter, Emma Mguni, returned home and together they now make bead-work articles for the tourist trade to supplement her husband's wages.

Sophie MGUNI page 30
Born about 1950 on Saaiplaas Farm near Groblersdal, she went to Wolwekraal in 1965. Her husband works in Pretoria and makes the 100 mile bus journey twice a day. Her most recent mural painted in 1979, is unusually figurative and contains the curious injunction, 'Eyes off!', that is, 'Don't look!'.

Sfiso MKAME page 76
Born on 6 May 1963 in Clermont Township outside Durban. He completed his higher-primary schooling at Roma School in Clermont and gained his Senior Certificate from Mtwaluma High School in 1980. In 1982 he joined the Open School in Durban where he studied printmaking under Richard Prestwich. He is an active member of the Clermont Youth League and has exhibited regularly at the Community Arts Workshop in Durban as well as in a number of group exhibitions in the Durban area.

Thamsanqwa MNYELE page 83
Born on 10 December 1948 in Alexandra Township, Johannesburg. Studied at the ELC Art and Craft Centre at Rorke's Drift in the 1970s. In 1979, while on a visit to Gaborone, he decided not to come back to South Africa. He helped form the Medu Art Ensemble. This arts organization operated workshops in graphics, photography, film, theatre, music and literature. In 1982 he helped organize the Culture and Resistance Festival. On 14 June 1985, less than a month after he had married, he was shot dead by members of the South African Defence Force during a raid on suspected members of the ANC living in the Botswana capital.

Nat MOKGOTSI page 81
Born in 1946 in Newclare Township, Johannesburg. Studied at the Jubilee Arts Centre (old Polly Street Centre). Now teaches art at the Open School in Johannesburg.

Melita MOLOKWANE page 57
Born on 26 September 1963 in Mokomene Township, Pietersburg. Completed her Junior Certificate in 1980 at the Mokomene High School. Before moving to her husband's parents' home at Syferfontein in the Mountain Hill district of Venda, Melita worked as a building labourer in Pietersburg.

Mboyi MOSHIDI pages 28, 71
Born in 1953 in Johannesburg. Attended watercolour classes at the Federated Union of Black Arts under Dumisani Mabaso. Now assistant printmaker at the Johannesburg Art Foundation.

Titus MOTEYANE page 41
Born on 12 March 1963 in Atteridgeville Township, Pretoria. He completed high school in 1983 when he formed a band with Joseph Chauke. Since then he has worked as a musician, as a packer and as a general labourer in an engineering company.

Emily Manini MOTSOENENG pages 54, 55
Born on 5 March 1918 on Horse-Hoek Farm in the Fauriesburg district. Motsoeneng completed her traditional African schooling in 1938 and learnt the art of wall painting from her mother. She writes: 'My mother taught me the art-training of painting, at the age of 20 years. All the girls of the village were taught and trained how to paint walls of huts internally and externally artistically. That was where we used to expose and reflect our talents and skills of art. We used different colours of water paint to decorate the walls, with our bare hands.'

Tommy MOTSWAI page 50
Born on 27 May 1963 in Rockville, Soweto. Attended higher-primary school at the Kutlwanong School for the Deaf. In 1986 he won a bursary to study art and attended workshops at FUBA. He is presently an art teacher at the Kutlwanong School.

George MSIMANG page 30
Born on 26 October 1948 in Lamontville Township, Durban. Completed secondary school education at Lamontville High School in 1968. Studied art at the ELC Art and Craft Centre at Rorke's Drift during 1969 and 1970. Thereafter at the Accademia di Belle Arti in Rome until 1975. In 1978 he was one of five artists commissioned by the Institute of Race Relations to produce murals on the walls of the Port Natal beer hall in Umlazi Township. Since then he has exhibited his work and published some of his sketches in local newspapers.

John Ndevasia MUAFANGEJO pages 7, 90
Born in 1943 at Etunda lo Nghadi, Angola. Attended school at St Mary's Mission at Odibo in the Owambo province of Namibia. In 1967 he entered the two-year art course at the ELC Art and Craft Centre at Rorke's Drift. After teaching at St Mary's Mission for five years he returned to Rorke's Drift for a refresher course in 1974. Since that time he has lived and worked in Katutura Township, Windhoek. He died at his home on 27 November 1987.

Nelson MUKHUBA page 46
Born on 22 August 1925 at Tshakhuma Village, Venda. Educated to the higher-primary school level before working as a labourer and handyman in various trades. During the 1960s he formed a marabi band, Nelson and the Phiri Boys, and recorded with the Zoutpansberg Merry Makers and the Music Men. He also formed a traditional dance troupe, Mahlombe a Muthandabinyuka. Since 1980 his wood carvings have attracted wide critical attention and they have been reproduced on the 'Republic' of Venda's postal stamps. He committed suicide in 1987.

Sam NHLENGETHWA page 77
Born on 9 January 1955 at Payneville Township, Springs. Studied art through the ELC Art and Craft Centre at Rorke's Drift. Now a set designer with TV 2, South African Broadcasting Corporation.

Derrick Vusimuzi NXUMALO page 52
Born in 1962 in the Dumisa area of Natal. Completed his secondary school education at Phindavela High School and found employment as a waiter at a hotel in Scottburgh. Later he worked as a gardener on the Berea in Durban and was recruited to work in the gold mines in 1986.

Madi PHALA page 70
Born on 2 February 1955 at Payneville Township, Springs. Studied at the Botswana Training College in Mafeking. He is presently an effects maker with the South African Broadcasting Corporation.

Johannes PHOKELA page 60
Born on 11 January 1966 in Soweto. Whilst completing his Junior Certificate he attended children's art classes at the Open School in Johannesburg and later completed a two-year Fine Art course at FUBA in 1986. He has exhibited in the annual student exhibitions at FUBA and is now studying at St Martin's School of Art in London.

Mpolokeng RAMPHOMANE page 64
Born on 4 April 1955 in Soweto, Johannesburg. Studied art informally at the YWCA in Dube and at the ELC Art and Craft Centre at Rorke's Drift.

Michele RAUBENHEIMER page 14
Born on 30 March 1957 in Cape Town, Raubenheimer completed all her schooling at the Waldorf School in Cape Town and matriculated there in 1974. She enrolled at the University of Stellenbosch but transferred to the University of Cape Town. After completing a degree in Fine Art in 1980, she worked for the South African Allied Workers' Union. In 1983 she returned to UCT to complete a post-graduate diploma, specializing in print-making. Currently she is teaching in the Fine Arts Department at the University of the Witwatersrand and completing her Master's Degree in Fine Art.

Mmakgabo Helen SEBIDI page 29
Born on 5 March 1943 at Skilpadfontein, Transvaal. Completed higher-primary schooling at Khutsong Primary School. Her grandmother taught her dressmaking and crochet skills and she received informal training from Koenafeela Mohl. She joined the Katlehong Art Centre at Natalspruit near Germiston where she studied ceramics. In 1987 she enrolled at the Johannesburg Art Foundation under Bill Ainslie.

Eunice Matshitiso SEFAKA page 14
Born on 2 August 1962 in Smithfield in the Orange Free State. After completing her Lower-Primary Certificate she gained her Junior Certificate at Mapoi High School in 1982. Sefaka joined the Community Arts Project the following year, and completed the two-year full-time course in 1986. The following year she qualified for a teacher's certificate at CAP and is now teaching there.

Phutuma SEOKA page 35
Born in 1922 at Mojaji, Lebowa. He did not attend school and worked on the Witwatersrand where he sold herbal remedies and patent medicines. His family was removed to Mamaila and he returned to look after his ailing father. On his return he established a barber's shop at the nearby village of Molototsi on the main road to Giyani where he continued to sell patent medicines. He and his sons began selling carvings on the side of the road in about 1976 and he achieved critical acclaim after the 1985 BMW Tributaries exhibition in Johannesburg. Since then his work has been the subject of a television documentary and he has exhibited regularly in galleries and shops specializing in African crafts.

Paul SIBISI pages 18, 72
Born in 1948 in Umkhumbane, Durban. In 1968 he studied at the Ndaleni Art School on a Bantu Education bursary and attended classes at the ELC Art and Craft Centre at Rorke's Drift during 1973 and 1974. Thereafter he took up a teaching post at Umzavela High School in Umlazi Township. In 1987 he was awarded a six-month British Council fellowship to study contemporary printmaking.

Robert Zithulele SIWANGAZA page 32
Born on 10 June 1962 in Zwelethemba Township, Worcester. Completed his secondary schooling at Vusisizwe High School in 1979. Worked as a casual labourer in the construction industry until the beginning of 1985 when he enrolled for the full-time art course at the Community Arts Project. He now teaches in the children's art programme.

Velile SOHA page 25
Born on 12 February 1956 in Somerset Strand, Western Cape. The family was removed to Nyanga in 1961 and his father was employed by the Township Administration Board. He received his primary school education at Tembani Lower-Primary and the Zimasa Higher-Primary Schools in Nyanga. Financial difficulties forced him to abandon high school and he worked for a while on the South African Railways. He was introduced to the Community Arts Project by Mpathi Gocini and in 1980 he was sent to the ELC Art and Craft Centre at Rorke's Drift. After completing his Fine Art Certificate in 1982 he worked in Johannesburg at Tony Nkotsi's studio. In 1984 he joined the Nyanga Arts Centre as a teacher.

Bernard M. TSHATSINDE page 59
Born about 1959 in Mamelodi Township, Pretoria. After attending local schools he completed a Fine Art degree through the University of Fort Hare in 1987. He now teaches art at a school near Alice, Ciskei.

Tito ZUNGU page 44
Born in about 1946 at Mapumulo, Natal. He did not attend school and worked as a farm hand until he came to Durban in 1966. Worked as a gardener before getting a job in a dairy in Pinetown. He drew from an early age and sold his first decorated envelope in 1960. Ten years later, his work was brought to the attention of Jo Thorpe at the African Art Centre and his work was first exhibited in 1971 in the Art SA Today exhibition. His work was reproduced in UCLA's *African Arts* magazine in 1972 and 1976. Now he works for the Dominican Sisters as a cook at the Walsingham Girls Club in Durban.

Glossary of Acronyms, Contractions and Colloquialisms

ANC — African National Congress
AZAPO — Azanian People's Organization
Buffel — armoured troop carrier
CAHAC — Cape Areas Housing Action Committee
CAP — Community Arts Project
CATA — Cape African Teachers' Association
CAYCO — Cape Youth Congress
Casspir — armoured personnel carrier
COSAS — Congress of South African Students
COSATU — Congress of South African Trade Unions
domba — female initiation rites practised by the Vhavenda people
ECC — End Conscription Campaign
FUBA — Federated Union of Black Arts
iingqayi — small, narrow necked clay vessels
isichumo — basketwork finely woven enough to contain liquid
JBMF — Johannesburg Bantu Music Festival
JMC — Joint Management Centre
jsuri — large carved wooden bowl used for pounding grain
lapa — low courtyard wall
mbaqanga — originally a popular form of African Jazz, the term is now applied to a new style of urban neo-traditional music played on modern electric instruments
NEAD — Non-European Affairs Department
NECC — National Education Crisis Committee
'Necklace' — method of killing a person by placing a used car tyre around the body before soaking it in petrol and setting light to it
NSA — Natal Society of Arts
NUSAS — National Union of South African Students
nyamisoro — carved wooden and beaded doll with detachable head disclosing cavity for the storing of medicine
PAC — Pan Africanist Congress
PCB — Publications Control Board
PUTCO — Public Utility and Transport Corporation
Reef Areas — towns along the ridge of the Witwatersrand below which there is a gold-bearing reef
RSC — Regional Services Councils
SA — South Africa
SAAA — South African Association of Arts
SABC — South African Broadcasting Corporation
SACC — South African Council of Churches
SACHED — South African Committee for Higher Education
SANSCO — South African National Students' Congress
SATS — South African Transport Services
SASO — South African Students' Organization
shebeen — illegal drinking house
sorgham — African millet
SPCC — Soweto Parents Crisis Committee
stokvel — a working-class credit association
TATA — Transvaal African Teachers' Association
TECON — Theatre Council of Natal
TLSA — Teachers' League of South Africa
tshefana — motif derived from the patterns on a safety razor blade
UCT — University of Cape Town
UDF — United Democratic Front
UWC — University of the Western Cape
WECSCO — Western Cape Schools Congress
WECTU — Western Cape Teachers' Union
WITS — University of the Witwatersrand,
Witwatersrand — industrial and gold-mining area

Author's Acknowledgments

My greatest debt is to the artists who gave up their time and offered me the hospitality of their homes. Among these, special mention should be made of David Koloane, Bongiwe Dhlomo, 'MK' Malefane, Paul Sibisi and Luthando Lupuwana, who also conducted some of the initial interviews. Many people gave me advice and introduced me to different artists. Among these people I must single out Anne Collins of ITSIDU, Fiona Nicholson and David Rousseau of Ditike, Jo Thorpe and Terry-Anne Stevenson of the African Art Centre, Alan Crump of the University of the Witwatersrand, Matsemela Manaka of Funda Centre, Hillary Graham of the University of Fort Hare, Lorna Ferguson of the Tatham Art Gallery and Bill Ainslie of the Johannesburg Art Foundation. The Friends of the South African National Gallery kindly allowed me to reproduce Tommy Motswai's *The Tea-party* and the Tatham Art Gallery allowed me to include the following works from their collection: Derrick Nxumalo's *Vaal Reefs* and Sfiso Mkame's *Letters to my Child*. Vanessa Solomon and Tshilidzi Ligege gave invaluable assistance as interpreters. Two of the artists' entries were first published, in slightly different form, in *ADA Magazine*. I am also indebted to Glenda Younge for her untiring help and rigorous scrutiny of the text at unreasonable hours of the night. Lastly, I wish to thank the University of Cape Town for granting me generous research leave and the Harry Oppenheimer Centre for African Studies and the University Research Committee for meeting a portion of my research costs.

Photographic Acknowledgments

All photographs were taken by the author except for those detailed below. I would like to take this opportunity to thank all those who generously allowed their photographs to be published in this volume: Michele Raubenheimer, p. 14 below (*Slugabed*); Paul Grendon, pp. 17, 19; Paul Sibisi, pp. 18, 72, 73; Patricia Davidson, p. 35 (Seoka's studio and 'gallery'); Bruce Campbell-Smith, p. 42 (Johannes Maswanganyi); The Durban African Art Centre, pp. 44, 45; Pamela Warne, pp. 46, 74, 78/79; Kathy Grundlingh, p. 50 (*The Tea-party*); Tatham Art Gallery, Pietermaritzberg, pp. 52, 76; Madi Phala, p. 71; Sam Nhlengethwa, p.77; Ronnie Levitan, p. 85 (*Seeing Straight*).